P9-DHF-619

WILLIAMS-SONOMA

Backyard Barbecues

GENERAL EDITOR
Chuck Williams

RECIPES
Phillip Stephen Schulz

PHOTOGRAPHY
Richard Eskite

TIME
LIFE
BOOKS

TIME-LIFE BOOKS
Time-Life Books is a division of Time Life Inc.
Time-Life is a trademark of Time Warner Inc. U.S.A.

TIME-LIFE CUSTOM PUBLISHING
Vice President and Publisher: Terry Newell
Vice President of Sales and Marketing: Neil Levin
Director of Financial Operations: J. Brian Birky
Director of Acquisitions: Jennifer L. Pearce

WILLIAMS-SONOMA
Founder and Vice-Chairman: Chuck Williams
Book Buyer: Victoria Kalish

WELDON OWEN INC.
President: John Owen
Vice President and Publisher: Wendely Harvey
Chief Operating Officer: Larry Partington
Vice President International Sales: Stuart Laurence
Associate Publisher: Lisa Atwood
Managing Editor: Jan Newberry
Consulting Editor: Norman Kolpas
Copy Editor: Sharon Silva
Design: Kari Perin, Perin+Perin
Production Director: Stephanie Sherman
Production Manager: Jen Dalton
Production Editor: Sarah Lemas
Food Stylist: Pouké
Prop Stylist: Laura Ferguson
Photo Production Coordinator: Juliann Harvey
Photo Assistant: Kevin Hossler
Food Styling Assistant: Jeff Tucker
Glossary Illustrations: Alice Harth

A NOTE ON WEIGHTS AND MEASURES
All recipes include customary U.S. and metric
measurements. Metric conversions are based on a
standard developed for these books and have been
rounded off. Actual weights may vary.

The Williams-Sonoma Lifestyles Series
conceived and produced by Weldon Owen Inc.
814 Montgomery Street, San Francisco, CA 94133

In collaboration with Williams-Sonoma
3250 Van Ness Avenue, San Francisco, CA 94109

Separations by Colourscan Overseas Co. Pte. Ltd.
Printed in Singapore by Tien Wah Press (Pte.) Ltd.

A WELDON OWEN PRODUCTION
Copyright © 1999 Weldon Owen Inc.
All rights reserved, including the right of
reproduction in whole or in part in any form.

First printed in 1999
10 9 8 7 6 5 4 3 2 1

Library of Congress
Cataloging-in-Publication Data

Schulz, Phillip Stephen.
Backyard barbecues / general editor, Chuck Williams;
  recipes by Phillip Stephen Schulz; photography by
  Richard Eskite.
        p. cm. — (Williams-Sonoma lifestyles)
    Includes index.
    ISBN 0-7370-2011-3
    1. Barbecue cookery. I. Williams, Chuck.
  II. Title. III. Series.
  TX840.B3B28 1999
  641.5'784— dc21   98-35958
                                        CIP

A NOTE ON NUTRITIONAL ANALYSIS
Each recipe is analyzed for significant nutrients per
serving. Not included in the analysis are ingredients
that are optional or added to taste, or are suggested
as an alternative or substitution either in the recipe
or in the recipe introduction or accompanying tip. In
recipes that yield a range of servings, the analysis is
for the middle of that range.

Contents

8 SETTING UP AN OUTDOOR KITCHEN

10 BUILDING A FIRE   12 SETTING UP A SMOKER

14 BEVERAGES   16 PLANNING MENUS

18 Poultry & Seafood

56 Beef, Pork & Lamb

74 Vegetables & Side Dishes

98 Desserts

108 GLOSSARY   112 INDEX

Welcome

"Come on over for a backyard barbecue" is always a welcome invitation. For me, as for so many other people, it brings to mind images of easy, casual conversation, bright midday sunshine or a cooling breeze at dusk, refreshing drinks in tall glasses, and hearty food seasoned with smoke.

This book dedicates itself to the pleasures of backyard barbecuing. It begins with a survey of all the essentials, from setting the outdoor dining scene and keeping beverages cold to step-by-step cooking instructions. The how-to demonstrations acknowledge that the word *barbecue* means different things to different people, including both relatively quick methods for outdoor grilling and more leisurely techniques for smoking foods—what purists call true barbecue.

Among the 49 recipes in this book, you'll find outstanding examples for both grilled and hot-smoked foods. There's also a generous selection of appetizers, salads, side dishes, and desserts suitable for rounding out menus, whether informal or grand. So, whether you're inviting friends over for a gala celebration or simply planning a casual family meal, this book has all the information you need to make your backyard barbecue a success.

Setting Up an Outdoor Kitchen

A successful backyard barbecuer has everything organized for an outdoor meal (right): a charcoal-fueled kettle-type grill in a clear, open space near a table covered with wipe-clean oilcloth. Keep long-handled utensils handy and have ready-to-grill ingredients close by, along with serving plates and a refreshing drink for the cook. For nighttime dining, candles (below) light the scene. Include some citronella tapers to keep bugs at bay.

Getting Organized

The most important piece of equipment in any outdoor kitchen is a grill (see pages 10–13). Find a convenient place for yours that's clear of potential fire hazards and well ventilated. A built-in counter, portable tables, or trays where you can keep tools, food, and serving platters or plates close by will cut down on trips back and forth to the kitchen.

Sturdy, long-handled cooking tools designed specifically for grilling let you work at a safe distance from the fire. Tongs, a two-pronged fork, and a spatula are a good basic set to have on hand. If you plan to make kabobs, you'll want a set of skewers. Grill baskets for easier handling of delicate foods like fish and vegetables are also useful (see glossary, page 108). A fine-mesh grill screen is used for foods likely to stick to the grill and to keep small foods from falling into the fire. Keep oven mitts or pot holders nearby to protect your hands from the heat.

Planning Food and Drink

At least a day beforehand, read over the recipes and do as much work as possible in advance. Make room in the refrigerator for foods that need to stay cold until cooked or served. Have clean platters ready to put food on after cooking, to avoid the risk of contamination from raw seafood, poultry, or meat juices.

Your work will go easier, too, if you round out the menu with items cooked ahead indoors. (This book includes recipes for many such classic accompaniments.)

You'll want to have a generous supply of prepared drinks (pages 14–15), wine, beer, and sodas on hand. Improvise a cooler from any container that can accommodate ice and bottles in quantity—washtubs, wading pools, or even a child's wagon. Brew coffee or tea ahead of time, and keep at serving temperature in a thermos.

Controlling the Environment

For daytime barbecues, make sure there's a refuge from the midday sun for the cook and the guests. Set the dining table and the cooking area in the shade of a tree or other shelter or beneath umbrellas or a canopy. At night, be sure to provide adequate lighting, using candles, small lanterns, hurricane lamps, or simple electric fixtures.

Of course, light draws garden pests, which are also irresistibly attracted to food and humans. Citronella, a citrusy oil extracted from the Asian grass of the same name, is a fairly effective, strong-smelling repellent available as candles or as oil for burning in lanterns or torches. Or consider burning Middle Eastern or Asian insect-repellent incense coils or cade oil extracted from a kind of juniper shrub, popular in the south of France.

You can even set the table with small pots or bouquets of plants that repel insects naturally, such as marigolds, lavender, rosemary, eucalyptus, or bay. Cover food with inexpensive mesh domes of wire, rattan, or plastic.

Cut down on traffic through the house by bringing what you need from the kitchen outdoors. Guests can help themselves to cold drinks from a wagon filled with ice (top, left). Enlist a serving tray for presenting cutlery, napkins, and cold drinks (top, right). A soup bowl holds the sauce for basting chicken on the grill (above).

Building a Fire

A fine coat of gray ash signals that the charcoal is ready for cooking. Use long-handled tongs to move the coals safely, forming an even bed on the fire grate for efficient direct-heat grilling.

Choosing a Fuel

Charcoal briquettes are the most popular fuel for outdoor grills. Although briquettes generally make a fine fire, some people think they leave an unpleasant aftertaste in food. Natural lump hardwood charcoal burns cleaner and at higher temperatures.

Gas grills, fueled by liquid propane sold in refillable canisters, produce a clean, hot flame. These grills usually include a bed of crushed lava rock or ceramic briquettes to retain the heat.

Starting the Fire

Generations of backyard barbecuers have lit their grills by building a pyramid of charcoal briquettes and soaking it with lighter fluid before igniting it with a match. While the pyramid efficiently conserves heat, lighter fluid—or presoaked charcoal briquettes—can be dangerous, contribute to air pollution, and can give food an unpleasant chemical taste. An electric fire starter or paraffin-saturated fire starters are safer, more sensible alternatives to lighter fluid.

One of the best tools for lighting coals is a chimney starter. Put this sheet-metal cylinder on the fire grate, stuff crumpled newspaper under it, pile charcoal on top, and ignite the newspaper.

When the coals are ready, they will be covered in pale gray ash; in the dark, they will glow red. This should take 25–30 minutes for a pyramid, or as little as 20 minutes with a chimney starter. Gas grills need about 15 minutes for their lava rocks or ceramic briquettes to build up heat.

Using Direct or Indirect Heat

Before you grill, you need to determine whether you'll be cooking with direct or indirect heat. The difference between the methods is determined by where the food is placed in relation to the fire.

The direct-heat method utilizes the direct heat of the fire. Use for searing and for grilling foods that take less than 25 minutes to cook, such as fish fillets or poultry, burgers, steaks, sausages, kabobs, or vegetables. These foods should be put on the grill directly over the coals or gas burners.

The indirect-heat method uses reflected heat to cook foods placed away from the fire. Use it for large cuts of meat and other foods that require longer cooking times at low temperatures. Indirect-heat cooking requires that the grill be kept covered. Every time you lift the lid, heat escapes, which can increase the cooking time.

There are several ways to control the fire in a charcoal grill. One way to increase the heat is to push the coals close together. Spreading them apart will bring the temperature down. You can also close the vents partially if your fire is burning too hot; open them all the way when you need more heat.

INDIRECT HEAT

CHARCOAL GRILL - In a kettle grill arranged for indirect-heat cooking, the lighted coals—here, lump hardwood charcoal—are pushed to the perimeter of the fire bed. In the cleared space, an aluminum-foil pan filled with water will catch drippings from food that will cook directly above it.

GAS GRILL - To prepare a gas grill for indirect-heat cooking, put a liquid-filled aluminum-foil pan directly beneath the rack where the food will cook. This will prevent any drippings from the food falling into the fire, which can cause flare-ups. Turn all the burners to high to preheat the grill for 10–15 minutes, then turn off any burners directly beneath the food and adjust the remaining burners to equal degrees of heat (high, medium, or low) as indicated in your recipes. Indirect-heat cooking allows heat to rise, reflect off the lid and grill surfaces, and cook the food from all sides. The heat circulates inside the grill, so turning the food is not necessary.

GRILL CARE

Because grills live outdoors, we tend to pay less attention to their care and cleaning than we do to indoor kitchen appliances. Backyard grills, however, can represent a significant investment worth preserving for many years, plus they work best when properly maintained.

Use a long-handled, wire-bristled brush to scrub food particles off the cooking grid while it is still hot. They will literally go up in smoke, and the grid will be easier to wash and dry later if there's no food baked onto it.

Always clean out the fire pan of a charcoal grill the day after you use it, at which point the coals will have cooled and be fully extinguished. Wash or hose down the inside to wash away any charcoal dust or soot that might otherwise settle on the food the next time you cook.

Sort through the lava rocks or ceramic briquettes of a gas grill after they have cooled completely to get rid of any food particles that might clog the gas jets. Occasionally a lava or ceramic bed gets too soiled and will no longer retain heat effectively. You will then need to replace it.

When not in use, protect your grill with a waterproof cover, and store it inside a roofed structure, if possible, to prevent rusting.

Setting Up a Smoker

Controlling Smoke, Moisture, and Low Heat

In a smoker, food cooks slowly, enveloped in a haze of smoke and sometimes also steam, at temperatures ranging from 180° to 250°F (82°–120°C)—conditions ideal for cooking large cuts of meat or whole poultry or fish.

Depending upon the size of the food being smoked, cooking may take 1½–8 hours. But little effort is required, and the results merit the wait, with food surpassingly tender, succulent, and aromatic with smoke.

There are two basic types of smokers. Relatively inexpensive water smokers generate moist heat suited to lean cuts of beef, pork tenderloins, or chicken. The resulting smoky flavor tends to be subtler than that produced in a dry smoker. For additional flavor, some cooks add seasonings such as bay leaves, rosemary, lemon slices, or peppercorns to the water pan, or sometimes even a flavorful liquid like beer.

Dry smokers cook without added steam and give foods a more intense, smoky flavor. If

WATER SMOKER

From bottom up, a water smoker features a fire pan, a water pan, one or more cooking grids, and a lid. A side door lets you add more fuel or wood without significant heat loss.

DRY SMOKER

A dry smoker features a fire box at one side, with a door for adding extra fuel or wood during cooking. On the opposite side, a vent draws heat and smoke to the cooking chamber.

moist heat is required, you can easily add a water pan to the fire box or cooking grid.

A temperature gauge on the smoker will let you know when to add more fuel to help maintain constant heat.

Building the Smoker Fire

Master smokers swear by all-wood fires. Most people, however, will find a combination of charcoal and wood easier to manage.

Always follow the manufacturer's instructions for starting and maintaining the fire. To generate smoke, add wood chips or chunks, available anywhere outdoor cooking supplies are sold.

Choose a fragrant nut or fruit wood (see some popular options, right) that best complements the food. Before adding the chips or chunks, soak them in water for 30–60 minutes so that they will smolder, generating more smoke.

SMOKING WITH A CHARCOAL GRILL

If you'd like to smoke foods but don't own a smoker, you can easily improvise one in a covered charcoal grill. The trick is to cook at as low a temperature as possible, generating steam along with the smoke (see photo, right). If your grill doesn't have a thermometer, slip the stem of a standard roasting thermometer through one of its vents. Keep the temperature between 180°F (82°C) and 250°F (120°C) by adjusting the vents and adding preheated fuel as necessary.

To prepare a charcoal grill for smoking, pile charcoal on each side of a large pan of water. Keep the grill covered. When you lift the lid, heat escapes, increasing the cooking time.

HICKORY - A classic. Robust, pungent, and woodsy. Pairs well with beef, pork, or poultry.

MESQUITE - A tangy, strong-tasting southwestern favorite. Best for more quickly cooked items.

APPLE - Mild and sweet. Good with seafood, poultry, or pork.

CHERRY - Sweet and fruity. Tends to darken meat's color. Complements beef, pork, lamb, or turkey.

OAK - Strong but pleasant taste. Ideal for beef, lamb, or game.

Beverages

Iced Tea Cooler

Tangy and refreshing, this cooler is partially made in advance. The ginger ale, however, must be added just before serving, so be sure it is well chilled.

4 cups (32 fl oz/1 l) brewed tea, cooled
1 cup (8 fl oz/250 ml) orange juice
1 cup (8 fl oz/250 ml) cranberry juice
2½ tablespoons lemon juice, or more to taste
4 teaspoons superfine (caster) sugar, or more to taste
3 cups (24 fl oz/750 ml) ginger ale, chilled
ice cubes
3 orange slices, halved

❀ In a large glass pitcher, combine the tea, orange juice, cranberry juice, 2½ tablespoons lemon juice, and 4 teaspoons sugar. Stir to mix well. Cover and refrigerate until well chilled.

❀ Just before serving, stir in the ginger ale. Taste for sweetness, adding more lemon juice or sugar if needed. Pour over ice cubes in tall glasses. Cut a slit in each half orange slice and rest it on a glass rim to decorate. Serve immediately.

SERVES 6

Red Wine Sangria

Make sangria with red or white wine and flavor it with virtually any fruit you like. An apple, for instance, or even 1 cup (4 oz/125 g) stemmed strawberries can be substituted for the peach used here.

1 bottle (24 fl oz/750 ml) full-bodied, dry red wine or white wine
3 tablespoons orange juice
2 tablespoons lemon juice
2 tablespoons Grand Marnier or other orange-flavored liqueur
3 tablespoons superfine (caster) sugar
1 lemon, thinly sliced and seeded
1 small orange, thinly sliced and seeded
1 peach, peeled, pitted, and cut into wedges
2 cups (16 fl oz/500 ml) club soda, or to taste, chilled
ice cubes

❀ In a large glass pitcher, combine the wine, orange juice, lemon juice, liqueur, sugar, lemon and orange slices, and peach wedges. Stir to mix well. Cover and refrigerate until well chilled.

❀ Just before serving, stir in the 2 cups (16 fl oz/500 ml) club soda and ice cubes. Taste and add more club soda if the mixture is too strong. Serve in wineglasses.

SERVES 6

Pineapple-Banana Licuado

The blended fruit drinks known as *licuados* are whipped up right on the spot in small shops throughout Mexico. Likewise, this version is best made just before serving.

4 tangerines or small oranges, chilled
4 cups (1½ lb/750 g) cubed pineapple
    (about ½ large pineapple), chilled
1 ripe banana, peeled and sliced
1 cup (8 fl oz/250 ml) low-fat milk
8 ice cubes, plus extra for serving
2 tablespoons lemon juice
1 teaspoon honey

❀ Juice the tangerines; you should have about 1 cup (8 fl oz/250 ml). In a blender or food processor, combine half of the juice, half of the pineapple cubes, half of the banana slices, and half of the milk. Process until very smooth. Add 4 of the ice cubes. Process until the ice is crushed and transfer to a pitcher.

❀ Add the remaining tangerine juice, pineapple cubes, banana slices, and milk to the blender or food processor. Process until very smooth. Add the lemon juice, honey, and the remaining 4 ice cubes. Process until the ice is crushed, then add to the pitcher and stir until well mixed. Pour over ice cubes in tumblers and serve.

SERVES 6

Sparkling Limeade

Serve this refreshing limeade when you need a change from the ubiquitous lemonade. Garnish with a slice or two of lime or kiwifruit in place of the mint sprigs, if desired.

½ cup (4 fl oz/125 ml) water
½ cup (4 oz/125 g) sugar
2 cups (16 fl oz/500 ml) lime juice
    (from about 14 large limes)
4 cups (32 fl oz/1 l) sparkling water
    or club soda, chilled
4 fresh mint sprigs, plus 6 sprigs
    (optional)
ice cubes

❀ In a small saucepan over high heat, make a sugar syrup by combining the water and sugar. Bring to a boil, stirring to dissolve the sugar. Boil for 1 minute. Remove from the heat and let cool.

❀ In a large glass pitcher, stir together the sugar syrup and the lime juice. Cover and refrigerate until well chilled.

❀ Add the sparkling water or club soda to the pitcher and stir to mix well. Garnish with 4 of the mint sprigs. Pour over ice cubes and decorate each glass with a mint sprig, if desired.

SERVES 6

Planning Menus

The recipes in this book were developed to complement one another, resulting in scores of different menus for nearly any occasion. The 10 examples here represent only a handful of the many possible combinations. When planning an outdoor meal, consider pairing recipes that can be prepared in advance in the kitchen with those that are grilled. Smoked foods, which take longer to cook, allow you plenty of time to prepare side dishes and desserts to complete the meal.

Country Barbecue

Baby Back Ribs
with Peach Sauce
PAGE 72

South Fork Corn Salad
PAGE 76

Old-fashioned Potato Salad
PAGE 89

Iced Tea Cooler
PAGE 14

Tuscan Grill

Cornish Hens with Olive Oil
and Rosemary
PAGE 33

Asparagus with
Parmesan Cheese
PAGE 75

Italian Plum Cake
PAGE 107

Rustic Vegetarian

Ratatouille on the Grill
PAGE 90

Rustic Grilled Potatoes
PAGE 94

Peach and Berry Shortcake
PAGE 99

Elegant Grilled Supper

Mushroom and
Spinach Salad
PAGE 81

Duck Breasts
with Black Cherry Sauce
PAGE 42

Lemon and Lime Tart
PAGE 103

Light Vegetarian Lunch

Stuffed Crookneck Squash
PAGE 93

Tossed Green Salad

Baguette

Strawberry-Raspberry
Sherbet
PAGE 100

Tropical Celebration

Pineapple-Banana Licuado
PAGE 15

Scallops and Papaya
with Mango Sauce
PAGE 45

Steamed Rice

Lemon and Lime Tart
PAGE 103

A Day at the Park

Deviled Turkey Burgers
PAGE 40

Midwestern Coleslaw
PAGE 86

Old-fashioned Potato Salad
PAGE 89

Sparkling Limeade
PAGE 15

Texan Hoedown

Smoked Brisket
with Spicy Soppin' Sauce
PAGE 56

Bourbon Baked Beans
PAGE 82

Corn Bread with Chorizo
PAGE 85

Red Wine Sangria
PAGE 14

Zesty Outdoor Dinner

Porterhouse Steak
with Sauce Rouille
PAGE 63

Grilled Summer Squash
with Green Sauce
PAGE 78

Peach and Berry Shortcake
PAGE 99

Family Picnic

Classic Barbecued Chicken
PAGE 46

Corn on the Cob
with Pepper Butter
PAGE 97

Peanut Butter Pie
with Mocha Crust
PAGE 104

Mixed Seafood Grill

PREP TIME: 45 MINUTES, PLUS
1 HOUR FOR MARINATING

COOKING TIME: 20 MINUTES,
PLUS PREPARING FIRE

INGREDIENTS

24 steamer clams, well scrubbed

24 mussels, well scrubbed and
debearded

2 tablespoons cornstarch (cornflour)

24 large shrimp (prawns), peeled
and deveined

2 tablespoons olive oil

2 teaspoons minced fresh basil

2 teaspoons snipped fresh chives

2 tablespoons unsalted butter,
at room temperature

4 teaspoons Hungarian hot paprika

½ teaspoon salt

½ teaspoon ground pepper

1½ lb (750 g) firm fish fillets such as
weakfish, haddock, snapper, or
pompano, about ½ inch (12 mm)
thick

2 large lemons, cut into wedges

fresh parsley sprigs

Serve this mixed grill over rice and accompany with Corn on the Cob with Pepper Butter (page 97) and a green salad. If you like, include a few soft-shell crabs or lobster tails on the grill.

SERVES 6

❂ Place the clams and mussels in separate large bowls and add cold water to cover generously. Stir 1 tablespoon cornstarch into each bowl. Let stand for 30 minutes, then drain and rinse under running cold water. Place the clams and mussels in separate pots of cold water and set aside.

❂ Meanwhile, place the shrimp in a large bowl and drizzle with the olive oil. Sprinkle with the basil and chives. Mix well, cover, and refrigerate for 45 minutes.

❂ In a small bowl, mix together the butter, paprika, salt, and pepper. Rub this mixture over both sides of the fish fillets and place in a shallow nonaluminum dish. Cover and refrigerate for 30 minutes. Remove the shrimp and the fish from the refrigerator 15 minutes before grilling.

❂ Prepare a hot fire for direct-heat cooking in a covered grill (see page 10). Position the grill rack 4–6 inches (10–15 cm) above the fire.

❂ Preheat an oven to 250°F (120°C). Thread the shrimp onto metal skewers. Drain the mussels and clams, discarding any that do not close to the touch. Place the mussels in a lightly oiled hinged grill basket.

❂ Place the clams around the edges of the rack. Cover the grill, open the vents, and cook for 5 minutes. Place the basket holding the mussels on the center of the rack, cover, and continue to cook until both the clams and mussels have opened, about 8 minutes longer. Transfer to a large, shallow heatproof serving dish, discarding any that did not open, and keep warm in the oven.

❂ Lightly oil the hinged grill basket and place the fish fillets in it. Set on the rack along with the skewered shrimp. Cook uncovered, turning once, until the shrimp have turned pink and the fish fillets are opaque throughout, about 3 minutes on each side.

❂ Transfer the fish and shrimp to the dish holding the clams and mussels. Garnish with the lemon wedges and parsley and serve.

NUTRITIONAL ANALYSIS PER SERVING: Calories 347 (Kilojoules 1,457); Protein 48 g; Carbohydrates 13 g; Total Fat 12 g; Saturated Fat 4 g; Cholesterol 182 mg; Sodium 484 mg; Dietary Fiber 0 g

Turkey Breast with Dried Cranberry Salsa

PREP TIME: 30 MINUTES, PLUS
6¾ HOURS FOR MARINATING

COOKING TIME: 1½ HOURS,
PLUS PREPARING FIRE

INGREDIENTS

1 bone-in whole turkey breast,
  about 5 lb (2.5 kg)

1 clove garlic, crushed

½ teaspoon salt

½ teaspoon ground pepper

¼ cup (2 oz/60 g) unsalted butter

½ cup (4 fl oz/125 ml) dry white wine

½ cup (4 fl oz/125 ml) water

CRANBERRY SALSA

1 large navel orange

1 cup (4 oz/125 g) dried cranberries

1 can (8 oz/250 g) pineapple slices
  in juice

12 cherry tomatoes, halved

1 small jalapeño chile, seeded and
  finely chopped

1 tablespoon lime juice

1 teaspoon snipped fresh chives

1 tablespoon chopped fresh cilantro
  (fresh coriander)

Turkey breasts are perfect for grilling. A breast will need to cook for 1½–2 hours, so charcoal users must add partially lit coals to the fire after the first 45 minutes.

SERVES 6

❀ Rub the turkey breast with the crushed garlic and then rub the salt and pepper into the skin. Cover and refrigerate for 6 hours or up to overnight. Remove from the refrigerator 45 minutes before grilling.

❀ In a small saucepan over medium-high heat, melt the butter. Add the wine and water and bring to a boil. Remove from the heat.

❀ Prepare a hot fire for indirect-heat cooking in a covered grill (see page 11). Position the grill rack 4–6 inches (10–15 cm) above the fire.

❀ Place the turkey breast, skin side up, on a poultry rack, and then set the rack on the grill rack directly over a drip pan. Cover the grill and open the vents halfway. Cook, basting occasionally with the butter-wine mixture, until an instant-read thermometer inserted into the thickest part of the breast away from the bone registers 170°F (77°C), about 1½ hours.

❀ Meanwhile, make the cranberry salsa: Using a small, sharp knife, cut a slice off the top and bottom of the orange to expose the flesh. Place the orange upright on a cutting board and thickly slice off the peel in strips, cutting around the contour of the orange to expose the flesh. Cut the orange crosswise into slices ¼ inch (6 mm) thick, and then cut each slice into sections. Transfer the pieces to a bowl and stir in the dried cranberries. Open the can of pineapple and drain the juice into the bowl. Cut the pineapple slices into small pieces and add to the bowl along with the tomatoes, jalapeño, lime juice, and chives. Stir to mix, cover, and refrigerate for 1 hour.

❀ Transfer the turkey breast to a cutting board. Cover loosely with aluminum foil and let stand for 10 minutes. Drain the salsa and transfer to a serving bowl. Add the cilantro to the salsa and toss to mix. Slice the breast across the grain and arrange on a warmed platter. Serve immediately. Pass the salsa at the table.

NUTRITIONAL ANALYSIS PER SERVING: Calories 641 (Kilojoules 2,692); Protein 75 g; Carbohydrates 25 g; Total Fat 25 g; Saturated Fat 9 g; Cholesterol 208 mg; Sodium 361 mg; Dietary Fiber 2 g

Grilled Fish Steaks with Tartar Sauce

PREP TIME: 15 MINUTES, PLUS
1 HOUR FOR MARINATING

COOKING TIME: 10 MINUTES,
PLUS PREPARING FIRE

INGREDIENTS

½ cup (4 fl oz/125 ml) olive oil

¼ cup (2 fl oz/60 ml) lemon juice

½ teaspoon finely grated lemon zest

1 small clove garlic, minced

½ teaspoon salt

¼ teaspoon ground pepper

¼ teaspoon chopped fresh oregano

4 fish steaks, each about 10 oz
    (315 g) and 1 inch (2.5 cm) thick

TARTAR SAUCE

½ cup (4 fl oz/125 ml) mayonnaise

2 tablespoons sour cream

¼ teaspoon Dijon mustard

1 small shallot, minced

1 small sour gherkin, chopped

2 teaspoons chopped fresh dill

⅛ teaspoon finely chopped fresh
    tarragon

dash of hot-pepper sauce

salt and ground pepper to taste

COOKING TIP: When grilling fish,
the standard rule for calculating
cooking time is to allow 10 minutes
for each inch (2.5 cm) of thickness.

Swordfish, tuna, shark, salmon, or monkfish steaks can be used in this recipe. You can use fillets as well, but because they are more fragile than steaks, you should put them in lightly oiled hinged grill baskets. Do not marinate the steaks or fillets for more than 1 hour, or they will become mushy.

SERVES 4

❋ In a small bowl, whisk together the olive oil, lemon juice, lemon zest, garlic, salt, pepper, and oregano. Spoon half of the mixture into a shallow nonaluminum dish just large enough to hold the fish steaks snugly in a single layer. Pat the fish steaks dry with paper towels and place in the dish. Spread the remaining olive oil mixture over the steaks. Cover and refrigerate for 45 minutes. Remove from the refrigerator 15 minutes before grilling.

❋ Meanwhile, make the tartar sauce: In a small bowl, whisk together the mayonnaise, sour cream, and mustard until smooth. Stir in the shallot, gherkin, dill, and tarragon. Add hot-pepper sauce and season with salt and pepper. Cover and refrigerate until serving.

❋ Prepare a hot fire for direct-heat cooking in a grill (see page 10). Position the grill rack 4–6 inches (10–15 cm) above the fire.

❋ Remove the fish steaks from the marinade, reserving the marinade. Place the fish steaks on the rack. Cook, turning once and basting with the reserved marinade, until the flesh is opaque throughout and firm to the touch, 4–5 minutes on each side.

❋ Transfer to warmed individual plates and serve immediately. Pass the tartar sauce at the table.

NUTRITIONAL ANALYSIS PER SERVING: Calories 763 (Kilojoules 3,201); Protein 51 g; Carbohydrates 3 g; Total Fat 60 g; Saturated Fat 11 g; Cholesterol 118 mg; Sodium 726 mg; Dietary Fiber 0 g

Tandoori Chicken Wings with Raita

PREP TIME: 40 MINUTES,
PLUS 24 HOURS FOR
MARINATING

COOKING TIME: 25 MINUTES,
PLUS PREPARING FIRE

INGREDIENTS

3 lb (1.5 kg) chicken wings, tips
removed

juice of 1 lime

½ cup (4 oz/125 g) plain yogurt

2 cloves garlic, chopped

1 teaspoon peeled and minced fresh
ginger

1 tablespoon Hungarian hot paprika

2 teaspoons salt

½ teaspoon ground cumin

½ teaspoon ground coriander

¼ teaspoon ground turmeric

pinch of ground allspice

RAITA

2 cucumbers, peeled, halved, seeded,
and finely chopped

½ teaspoon salt

½ teaspoon red wine vinegar

¼ teaspoon sugar

½ cup (4 oz/125 g) plain yogurt

1 teaspoon snipped fresh chives

PREP TIP: Just before grilling, brush
the wings with ½ teaspoon red food
coloring diluted with ¼ teaspoon
water to give them the orange hue
of authentic tandoori.

Serve these wings on a party buffet or as appetizers for an informal dinner. They are also a good light meal on their own.

SERVES 4

❀ Place the wings in a large nonaluminum bowl, sprinkle with the lime
juice, and set aside.

❀ In a food processor, combine the yogurt, garlic, ginger, paprika, salt,
cumin, coriander, turmeric, and allspice. Process until smooth. Pour
over the chicken wings, then turn to coat. Cover and refrigerate for
24 hours. Remove from the refrigerator 30 minutes before grilling.

❀ To make the raita, place the cucumbers in a sieve set over a bowl and
sprinkle with the salt, vinegar, and sugar. Let stand for 15 minutes.
Press lightly with the back of a wooden spoon to release excess liquid,
then transfer to a clean bowl. Add the yogurt and chives, mix well,
cover, and refrigerate until serving.

❀ Prepare a hot fire (medium-hot if the grill basket sits flat on the rack)
for direct-heat cooking in a covered grill (see page 10). Position the grill
rack 4–6 inches (10–15 cm) above the fire.

❀ Lightly oil a hinged grill basket. Remove the chicken wings from the
marinade and place in the basket. Set the basket on the grill rack, cover
the grill, and open the vents. Cook, turning once, until the skin is crisp
and the juices run clear when a wing is pierced, about 25 minutes total.
If the wings are browning too quickly, close the vents.

❀ Transfer to a warmed platter and serve hot. Pass the raita at the table.

NUTRITIONAL ANALYSIS PER SERVING: Calories 421 (Kilojoules 1,768); Protein 38 g;
Carbohydrates 8 g; Total Fat 26 g; Saturated Fat 7 g; Cholesterol 111 mg; Sodium 1,015 mg;
Dietary Fiber 1 g

Smoked Chicken and Fennel Salad with Almonds

PREP TIME: 30 MINUTES,
PLUS 25 HOURS FOR
MARINATING AND DRYING

COOKING TIME: 1½ HOURS,
PLUS PREPARING FIRE

INGREDIENTS

SMOKED CHICKEN BREASTS

6 tablespoons (3 oz/90 g) coarse salt

2 tablespoons brown sugar

2 teaspoons five-spice powder

2 teaspoons Hungarian hot paprika

2 large whole chicken breasts, about
   2 lb (1 kg) each, split

SALAD

¼ cup (1¼ oz/37 g) slivered blanched
   almonds

2 fennel bulbs, about 1¼ lb (625 g)
   total weight

1 large shallot, minced

1 cup (8 fl oz/250 ml) mayonnaise

1 tablespoon finely grated lemon
   zest

½ teaspoon Dijon mustard

salt and ground pepper to taste

about 18 red leaf or butter (Boston)
   lettuce leaves

COOKING TIP: Fruit woods such as apple and peach create a particularly aromatic smoke that complements chicken. Hickory and mesquite are also good, but go easy with these, as they can overpower delicate foods.

These chicken breasts can be cooked over indirect heat on a regular charcoal grill if you don't have a smoker. It's difficult to maintain low temperatures in a regular grill, however, and you will need to add more coals as the chicken cooks. A gas grill is not recommended, as it is almost impossible to maintain the necessary low heat.

SERVES 6

❀ To prepare the chicken breasts, in a small bowl, combine the salt, brown sugar, five-spice powder, and paprika. Rinse the chicken breasts, pat dry, and then rub the breasts with the spice mixture. Place in a non-aluminum dish, cover, and refrigerate for 24 hours. Lightly rinse the spice mixture off the chicken breasts and pat dry with paper towels. Place the breasts on a rack and allow to air-dry for 1 hour.

❀ Prepare a low-heat fire in a dry smoker (see page 12). (Charcoal grill users will need to add more preheated coals after 40 minutes to maintain a constant temperature.) Place the chicken breasts on the highest rack. Cover and smoke, keeping the temperature between 165°F (74°C) and 180°F (82°C), until the breasts are firm to the touch and the juices run clear, about 1½ hours. Cool, remove the meat from the bones, and cut into strips about 1 inch (2.5 cm) long and ¼ inch (6 mm) wide.

❀ To make the salad, preheat an oven to 350°F (180°C). Spread the almonds on a baking sheet and toast until golden and fragrant, 5–7 minutes. Remove from the oven and let cool.

❀ Meanwhile, cut off the stems and feathery tops and any bruised outer stalks from the fennel bulbs. Chop the bulbs, then chop enough of the feathery tops to yield 1 tablespoon. Place the chopped fennel bulbs, chicken, shallot, and almonds in a bowl. Toss to mix.

❀ In a large bowl, whisk together the mayonnaise, lemon zest, and mustard until smooth. Add the fennel-chicken mixture and mix well. Season with salt and pepper. Cover and refrigerate for 30 minutes.

❀ Line 6 serving plates with the lettuce leaves. Spoon the fennel-chicken mixture on top. Sprinkle with the chopped fennel tops and serve.

NUTRITIONAL ANALYSIS PER SERVING: Calories 522 (Kilojoules 2,192); Protein 33 g; Carbohydrates 8 g; Total Fat 40 g; Saturated Fat 7 g; Cholesterol 104 mg; Sodium 625 mg; Dietary Fiber 2 g

Cornish Hens with Olive Oil and Rosemary

PREP TIME: 20 MINUTES,
    PLUS 37 HOURS FOR
    MARINATING

COOKING TIME: 25 MINUTES,
    PLUS PREPARING FIRE

INGREDIENTS

4 Cornish hens, 1–1¼ lb (500–625 g) each

1 cup (8 fl oz/250 ml) extra-virgin olive oil

2 teaspoons coarse ground black pepper

1 teaspoon coarse salt

1 teaspoon chopped fresh rosemary or ½ teaspoon dried rosemary

½ teaspoon cayenne pepper

¼ cup (2 fl oz/60 ml) lemon juice

A good quality extra-virgin olive oil is a must for this recipe, as the hens take on the flavor of the oil as they marinate. Do not stint on the long marination; it's essential for the most tender, flavorful bird. Polenta, topped with Ratatouille on the Grill (page 90), makes the perfect accompaniment.

SERVES 4

❀ Place each hen, breast side down, on a work surface. With heavy-duty kitchen scissors, cut from the neck to the tail along both sides of the backbone; discard the backbone. Trim any excess fat, turn breast side up, tuck in the wings, and press down firmly on the breastbone to flatten the bird.

❀ Pour ½ cup (4 fl oz/125 ml) of the olive oil into 2 nonaluminum dishes large enough to hold the hens flat, dividing the oil evenly. Place the hens in the oil, skin sides down. Pour the remaining ½ cup (4 fl oz/125 ml) oil over the hens, making sure they are entirely coated. Use a brush, if necessary, to coat evenly. Cover with plastic wrap and place a heavy weight on top of each hen. Refrigerate for 36 hours.

❀ In a small bowl, stir together the black pepper, salt, rosemary, and cayenne pepper. Remove the hens from the oil and sprinkle the pepper mixture evenly over both sides of each hen. Rub the mixture into the hens and then sprinkle them with the lemon juice. Cover and let stand at room temperature for 1 hour.

❀ Prepare a hot fire for direct-heat cooking in a covered grill (see page 10). Position the grill rack 4–6 inches (10–15 cm) above the fire.

❀ Place the hens, skin sides down, on the rack. Cover the grill and open the vents. Cook until the undersides are browned and crisp, about 15 minutes. (If the skin is not crisp enough at this point, remove the cover briefly.) Turn over the hens, cover, and continue to cook until nicely browned on the second sides and the juices run clear when a thigh is pierced at the thickest point, about 15 minutes longer.

❀ Transfer the hens to individual serving plates and serve.

NUTRITIONAL ANALYSIS PER SERVING: Calories 687 (Kilojoules 2,885); Protein 48 g; Carbohydrates 2 g; Total Fat 53 g; Saturated Fat 13 g; Cholesterol 283 mg; Sodium 510 mg; Dietary Fiber 0 g

Malaysian-Style Chicken with Satay Sauce

PREP TIME: 50 MINUTES,
PLUS 2½ HOURS FOR
MARINATING

COOKING TIME: 10 MINUTES,
PLUS PREPARING FIRE

INGREDIENTS

I can (14 fl oz/440 ml) "lite"
coconut milk

I teaspoon peeled and minced
fresh ginger

2 whole boneless, skinless chicken
breasts, about I½ lb (750 g) total
weight, cut into I-inch (2.5-cm)
pieces

SATAY SAUCE
2 small dried chiles, seeded and
chopped

¼ cup (2 fl oz/60 ml) hot water

2 tablespoons peanut oil

I small yellow onion, chopped

I clove garlic, chopped

I tablespoon soy sauce

I teaspoon ground turmeric

I cup (5 oz/155 g) dry-roasted
peanuts

I tablespoon lemon juice

Look for canned coconut milk in the Asian or ethnic foods section of your market. If the sauce becomes too thick, thin it with a little hot water.

SERVES 4 AS AN APPETIZER

❁ In a nonaluminum bowl, combine half of the coconut milk (a little less than I cup/8 fl oz/250 ml) and the ginger. Add the chicken pieces and turn to coat evenly. Cover and refrigerate for 2 hours. Remove from the refrigerator 30 minutes before grilling.

❁ Soak 8 wooden skewers in water to cover for 20–30 minutes.

❁ Meanwhile, make the satay sauce: In a small bowl, combine the chiles and hot water. Let stand for about 20 minutes.

❁ While the chiles are soaking, in a small frying pan over medium-low heat, warm the peanut oil until hot but not smoking. Add the onion and sauté until slightly wilted, about I minute. Add the garlic and sauté until fragrant, about 2 minutes. Then add the soy sauce and turmeric and continue to cook, stirring occasionally, until the onion is soft, 4–5 minutes longer. Remove from the heat and let cool.

❁ In a food processor, using on-off pulses, grind the peanuts coarsely; do not process to a paste. Transfer to a bowl and set aside. Add the soaked chiles along with 3 tablespoons of the soaking liquid to the food processor and process until smooth. Add the onion-garlic mixture and again process until smooth. Add the remaining coconut milk (scant I cup/ 8 fl oz/250 ml), the ground nuts, and the lemon juice and, using on-off pulses, process just until mixed. Transfer to a heatproof bowl. Place over (not touching) barely simmering water and cook, stirring occasionally, until hot, about 15 minutes. Keep warm until serving.

❁ Prepare a hot fire for direct-heat cooking in a grill (see page 10). Position the grill rack 4–6 inches (10–15 cm) above the fire.

❁ Meanwhile, drain the chicken and thread the pieces onto the skewers.

❁ Place the skewers on the rack. Grill, turning once, until the chicken is cooked through, 4–5 minutes on each side.

❁ Transfer to a platter and serve hot. Pass the sauce at the table.

NUTRITIONAL ANALYSIS PER SERVING: Calories 518 (Kilojoules 2,176); Protein 48 g; Carbohydrates 14 g; Total Fat 30 g; Saturated Fat 7 g; Cholesterol 99 mg; Sodium 391 mg; Dietary Fiber 4 g

Coconut Shrimp with Lime

PREP TIME: 15 MINUTES, PLUS
1 HOUR FOR MARINATING

COOKING TIME: 10 MINUTES,
PLUS PREPARING FIRE

INGREDIENTS

3 limes

½ cup (2 oz/60 g) dried flaked
    coconut

½ cup (4 fl oz/125 ml) milk

¼ cup (2 fl oz/60 ml) golden rum

1 tablespoon honey

24 extra-large shrimp (prawns),
    peeled and deveined

1 red (Spanish) onion, cut into ¾-inch
    (2-cm) pieces

2 tablespoons olive oil

½ teaspoon chopped fresh tarragon

PREP TIP: For a more formal presen-
tation, butterfly the shrimp before
marinating, in which case the
shrimp should be grilled in a lightly
oiled hinged grill basket. To butterfly
each shrimp, simply deepen the slit
made for deveining, taking care not
to cut all the way through, and then
flatten like an open book.

If you lose some of the coating as you skewer the shrimp, simply spoon on more before grilling. The shrimp also make great
appetizers, in which case the recipe will serve 6. Serve with
basmati rice and plenty of ice-cold beer.

SERVES 4

❀ Cut 1 lime in half lengthwise, then cut crosswise into thin slices.
Set aside. Grate enough zest from the remaining 2 limes to measure
1 teaspoon, then halve the limes and squeeze the juice from them.

❀ In a food processor, combine the coconut, milk, rum, and honey.
Process until the coconut is finely chopped but not puréed. Transfer
to a large nonaluminum bowl and stir in the lime juice, lime zest, and
the shrimp. Mix well. Cover and refrigerate for 45 minutes. Remove
from the refrigerator 15 minutes before grilling. If using wooden skewers,
soak 6–8 of them in water to cover for 20–30 minutes.

❀ Meanwhile, in a bowl, combine the onion, olive oil, and tarragon. Mix
well, cover, and set aside.

❀ Prepare a medium-hot fire for direct-heat cooking in a grill (see page 10).
Position the grill rack 4–6 inches (10–15 cm) above the fire.

❀ Remove the shrimp from the marinade, taking care not to knock off
any of the clinging marinade. Bend each shrimp almost in half and
insert a skewer just above the tail so it passes through the body twice.
Alternate the shrimp with the lime slices and onion pieces.

❀ Place the skewers on the rack. Cook, turning once, until the shrimp are
crisp on the outside and opaque throughout, 4–5 minutes on each side.

❀ To serve, remove the shrimp, lime slices, and onion pieces from the
skewers and place on a serving platter. Serve hot.

NUTRITIONAL ANALYSIS PER SERVING: Calories 255 (Kilojoules 1,071); Protein 21 g;
Carbohydrates 13 g; Total Fat 11 g; Saturated Fat 4 g; Cholesterol 148 mg; Sodium 174 mg;
Dietary Fiber 1 g

Tangy Salmon Steaks

PREP TIME: 10 MINUTES, PLUS
1 HOUR FOR MARINATING

COOKING TIME: 10 MINUTES

INGREDIENTS

¼ cup (2 oz/60 g) Dijon mustard

¼ cup (2 fl oz/60 ml) soy sauce

2 tablespoons dark brown sugar

1 small clove garlic, minced

pinch of ground cloves

4 salmon steaks, each about 10 oz
   (315 g) and 1 inch (2.5 cm) thick

PREP TIP: Thick salmon fillets with
the skin intact can be substituted for
the steaks. The skin helps to keep
the fish from falling apart, but a
hinged grill basket is recommended
for easy handling.

A pinch of ground cloves brings out the full flavor of the sweet, mustardy marinade. Serve with Corn on the Cob with Pepper Butter (page 97), sliced tomatoes, and a green salad.

SERVES 4

❀ In a small bowl, stir together the mustard, soy sauce, brown sugar, garlic, and cloves. Spread half the mixture over the bottom of a shallow nonaluminum dish just large enough to hold the salmon steaks snugly.

❀ Pat the salmon steaks dry with paper towels and place in the dish. Spread the remaining mustard mixture over the salmon, cover, and refrigerate for 45 minutes. Remove from the refrigerator 15 minutes before grilling.

❀ Prepare a hot fire for direct-heat cooking in a grill (see page 10). Position the grill rack 4–6 inches (10–15 cm) above the fire.

❀ Place the fish steaks on the rack. Cook, turning once, until the fish is opaque throughout and firm to the touch, 4–5 minutes on each side.

❀ Transfer to warmed individual plates and serve immediately.

NUTRITIONAL ANALYSIS PER SERVING: Calories 508 (Kilojoules 2,134); Protein 51 g; Carbohydrates 8 g; Total Fat 27 g; Saturated Fat 5 g; Cholesterol 147 mg; Sodium 1,539 mg; Dietary Fiber 0 g

Deviled Turkey Burgers

PREP TIME: 15 MINUTES

COOKING TIME: 12 MINUTES,
   PLUS PREPARING FIRE

INGREDIENTS

1⅓ lb (655 g) ground (minced) turkey

2 small green (spring) onions, finely
   chopped

2 teaspoons Dijon mustard

1 egg white, lightly beaten

¼ teaspoon salt

¼ teaspoon ground pepper

4 hamburger buns or rolls, split

4 lettuce leaves

4 large tomato slices

PREP TIP: For the juiciest, most flavorful burgers, be sure your ground
turkey includes both white and dark
meat. Turkey labeled "all white
meat" will be drier as well as more
expensive.

Turkey burgers have gotten a bad rap over the years, but when properly prepared, they can be just as juicy and tasty as beef burgers, especially when cooked on a grill and served with corn on the cob, coleslaw, and potato salad. Be sure to include all of your favorite hamburger condiments.

SERVES 4

❈ In a bowl, combine the turkey, green onions, mustard, egg white, salt, and pepper. Mix well and shape into 4 patties each about ⅔ inch (1.5 cm) thick.

❈ Prepare a hot fire for direct-heat cooking in a grill (see page 10). Position the grill rack 4–6 inches (10–15 cm) above the fire.

❈ Place the burgers on the rack. Cook, turning once, until firm to the touch, about 6 minutes on each side. Just before the burgers are done, place the buns or rolls, cut sides down, around the edges of the rack and toast lightly.

❈ Transfer the buns or rolls, cut sides up, to individual plates and top the bottom half of each with a lettuce leaf, a tomato slice, and then a burger. Serve immediately.

NUTRITIONAL ANALYSIS PER SERVING: Calories 389 (Kilojoules 1,634); Protein 32 g; Carbohydrates 23 g; Total Fat 17 g; Saturated Fat 5 g; Cholesterol 76 mg; Sodium 552 mg; Dietary Fiber 1 g

Duck Breasts with Black Cherry Sauce

PREP TIME: 10 MINUTES,
PLUS 2½ HOURS FOR
MARINATING

COOKING TIME: 30 MINUTES,
PLUS PREPARING FIRE

INGREDIENTS

2 boneless whole duck breasts,
about 1¾ lb (875 g) each

¼ cup (2 fl oz/60 ml) olive oil

¼ cup (2 fl oz/60 ml) orange juice

½ teaspoon peeled and minced fresh
ginger

½ teaspoon salt

¼ teaspoon red pepper flakes

BLACK CHERRY SAUCE

1 jar (12 oz/375 g) black cherry
preserves

½ cup (4 fl oz/125 ml) bottled chili
sauce

½ cup (4 fl oz/125 ml) beef broth

1 tablespoon hoisin sauce

½ teaspoon Dijon mustard

1 tablespoon snipped fresh chives

Available at many high-quality butcher shops, boneless duck breasts are ideally suited for grilling—the perfect way to eliminate some of their fat. Serve the duck rosy pink, drizzled with the savory cherry sauce.

SERVES 4

❈ Cut each duck breast in half. Using a sharp knife, cut several long slashes in the skin, taking care not to cut through to the meat. Place the breasts in a shallow nonaluminum dish just large enough to hold them in a single layer.

❈ In a small bowl, stir together the olive oil, orange juice, ginger, salt, and pepper flakes. Spoon half of the oil mixture over the duck breasts. Turn over the breasts and spoon the remaining marinade over the top. Cover and refrigerate, turning the breasts several times, for 2 hours. Remove from the refrigerator 30 minutes before grilling.

❈ Meanwhile, make the sauce: In a saucepan over medium-low heat, combine the cherry preserves, chili sauce, beef broth, hoisin sauce, and mustard. Stir well and bring to a boil. Reduce the heat to low, cover partially, and simmer until thickened, about 20 minutes. Remove from the heat.

❈ Prepare a hot fire for direct-heat cooking in a grill (see page 10). Position the grill rack 4–6 inches (10–15 cm) above the fire.

❈ Place the duck breasts, skin sides down, on the rack. Cook until the skin is crisp, about 5 minutes. Turn over the breasts and continue to cook until medium-rare, about 3 minutes longer. To test, press the meat; it will give slightly, then bounce back. Brush both sides of the breasts with a little of the black cherry sauce and grill for 1 minute on each side to glaze. Transfer the breasts to a cutting board, cover loosely with aluminum foil, and let stand for 5 minutes. Meanwhile, reheat the cherry sauce over low heat.

❈ Carve the duck breasts on the diagonal across the grain into thin slices. Arrange on a warmed platter and spoon the hot cherry sauce over the top. Sprinkle with the chives and serve at once.

NUTRITIONAL ANALYSIS PER SERVING: Calories 932 (Kilojoules 3,914); Protein 76 g; Carbohydrates 67 g; Total Fat 40 g; Saturated Fat 10 g; Cholesterol 411 mg; Sodium 1,084 mg; Dietary Fiber 1 g

Turkey-Stuffed Peppers

PREP TIME: 45 MINUTES

COOKING TIME: 55 MINUTES,
PLUS PREPARING FIRE

INGREDIENTS

6 green bell peppers (capsicums)

10 oz (315 g) Italian-style turkey sausage, casings removed

1 yellow onion, finely chopped

1 clove garlic, minced

1 tablespoon curry powder

½ teaspoon ground pepper

¼ teaspoon salt

2 eggs, lightly beaten

⅓ cup (3 fl oz/80 ml) rich chicken broth

1½ cups (7½ oz/235 g) cooked white rice

3 tablespoons fine dried bread crumbs

2 tablespoons grated Parmesan cheese

1 tablespoon olive oil

COOKING TIP: If the peppers do not brown nicely during grilling, place them on a baking sheet and slip under a preheated broiler (griller) for a few minutes to brown the tops.

These Italian-influenced peppers are wonderful hot off the grill or served at room temperature, drizzled with olive oil and vinegar. For a spicier dish, use half hot and half sweet sausages. When selecting peppers, choose short, squat ones that stand up on their own.

SERVES 6

❋ Cut a slice off the top of each pepper and remove the seeds. Bring a large saucepan three-fourths full of water to a boil. Add the bell peppers and blanch for 1 minute. Drain well and set aside.

❋ In a frying pan over medium heat, cook the sausage, breaking up the lumps with a wooden spoon, until the meat begins to lose its pink color, about 5 minutes. Add the onion, garlic, curry powder, pepper, and salt and cook, stirring frequently, until the onion is soft, about 10 minutes. Transfer to a bowl and let cool slightly.

❋ Add the eggs to the sausage mixture and mix well. Stir in the chicken broth and rice and again mix well.

❋ Spoon the sausage mixture into the peppers, dividing it evenly. Sprinkle the tops with the bread crumbs, Parmesan cheese, and olive oil, again dividing evenly.

❋ Prepare a hot fire for direct-heat cooking in a covered grill (see page 10). Position the grill rack 4–6 inches (10–15 cm) above the fire.

❋ Place the peppers on the grill rack. Cover the grill and open the vents halfway. Cook until the peppers are tender when pierced with a knife, about 40 minutes. If the peppers start to burn on the bottom, move them to the outer edges of the rack.

❋ Transfer the peppers to individual plates and serve hot.

NUTRITIONAL ANALYSIS PER SERVING: Calories 227 (Kilojoules 953); Protein 13 g; Carbohydrates 22 g; Total Fat 10 g; Saturated Fat 3 g; Cholesterol 97 mg; Sodium 544 mg; Dietary Fiber 2 g

Cloaked Fish Stuffed with Bok Choy

PREP TIME: 25 MINUTES

COOKING TIME: 20 MINUTES,
  PLUS PREPARING FIRE

INGREDIENTS

1½ lb (750 g) bok choy

2 tablespoons plus 2 teaspoons
  olive oil

I small clove garlic, minced

½ teaspoon peeled and minced fresh
  ginger

I large fresh shiitake mushroom,
  about 2 oz (60 g), stem discarded
  and cap halved and sliced

⅓ cup (about 2 oz/60 g) chopped
  prosciutto

I small carrot, peeled and grated

¼ cup (2 fl oz/60 ml) plus I tablespoon chicken broth

I tablespoon soy sauce

I tablespoon cornstarch (cornflour)

4 whole fish, about 1⅓ lb (655 g)
  each, boned (see note)

salt and ground pepper to taste

8 or more large butter (Boston) or
  iceberg lettuce leaves

Red snapper, black sea bass, trout, tilapia, whitefish, and whiting are excellent candidates for this unusual recipe.

SERVES 4

❋ Trim the bok choy leaves from their stems. Chop the leaves; cut each stem lengthwise into 2 or 3 strips and then slice crosswise into pieces.

❋ In a frying pan over medium heat, warm 2 tablespoons of the olive oil. Add the garlic and ginger and cook, stirring, until fragrant, about I minute. Add the mushroom, prosciutto, bok choy stems, carrot, and the ¼ cup (2 fl oz/60 ml) chicken broth. Cook, tossing constantly, until the bok choy is almost tender, about 3 minutes. Add the bok choy leaves and the soy sauce and cook, tossing constantly, until the leaves begin to wilt, about 30 seconds. Reduce the heat to low.

❋ In a small bowl, whisk together the cornstarch and the I tablespoon chicken broth until the cornstarch dissolves. Stir into the bok choy mixture and cook, stirring constantly, until the sauce is thickened, about 30 seconds. Remove from the heat and let cool.

❋ Prepare a hot fire for direct-heat cooking in a covered grill (see page 10). Position the grill rack 4–6 inches (10–15 cm) above the fire. Soak about 6 feet (2 m) kitchen string in water to cover for at least 15 minutes.

❋ Sprinkle the fish generously with salt and pepper. Lay 2 lettuce leaves, slightly overlapping, on a work surface. Place a fish on top and spoon one-fourth of the bok choy mixture into the fish cavity. Fold the leaves tightly over the fish (use another leaf if necessary). Place the fish in a lightly oiled hinged grill basket or tie in several places with the soaked kitchen string. Repeat with the remaining fish, stuffing, and leaves. Brush the fish packets with the 2 teaspoons olive oil.

❋ Place the fish on the grill rack. Cover the grill and open the vents. Cook until the lettuce is well browned on the underside, 5–7 minutes. Turn and continue to cook until the fish is opaque throughout at the thickest point (cut through the lettuce to test), 5–7 minutes longer.

❋ Transfer the fish to warmed individual plates and snip the strings, if used. Let diners open their own packets and discard the leaves.

NUTRITIONAL ANALYSIS PER SERVING: Calories 662 (Kilojoules 2,780); Protein 77 g; Carbohydrates 53 g; Total Fat 17 g; Saturated Fat 3 g; Cholesterol 128 mg; Sodium 1,054 mg; Dietary Fiber 17 g

Monkfish with Chipotle Sauce

PREP TIME: 15 MINUTES, PLUS
1 HOUR FOR MARINATING

COOKING TIME: 30 MINUTES,
PLUS PREPARING FIRE

INGREDIENTS

CHIPOTLE SAUCE

1 tablespoon olive oil

2 cloves garlic

1 canned chipotle chile in adobo
sauce

¼ cup (1½ oz/45 g) bottled chopped
roasted red pepper

⅔ cup (5 fl oz/150 ml) mayonnaise

3 tablespoons sour cream

3 tablespoons milk, or as needed

1 teaspoon lime juice

¼ teaspoon salt

2 tablespoons olive oil

2 tablespoons lime juice

2 teaspoons Hungarian sweet paprika

½ teaspoon salt

¼ teaspoon ground pepper

2½–3 lb (1.25–1.5 kg) monkfish
fillets, about 1 inch (2.5 cm) thick

Chipotle chiles are often sold canned in adobo sauce, a tart, spicy tomato-based concoction, in Latin American markets and many specialty-food stores. This recipe calls for monkfish, but any full-flavored fish (Chilean sea bass, for example) that can stand up to the spicy sauce will work well.

SERVES 6

❀ To make the sauce, in a small saucepan over low heat, warm the olive oil for 1 minute. Add the garlic cloves, cover tightly, and cook, stirring occasionally, until lightly golden and soft, about 20 minutes. Do not allow the garlic to burn. Remove from the heat and let cool.

❀ In a food processor, combine the cooked garlic and oil, the chipotle chile, the red pepper, and ⅓ cup (2½ fl oz/75 ml) of the mayonnaise. Process until smooth. Add the remaining ⅓ cup (2½ fl oz/75 ml) mayonnaise, the sour cream, milk, lime juice, and salt. Process until smooth, adding another tablespoon or so of milk if needed to achieve a light and creamy sauce. Transfer to a bowl, cover, and refrigerate until serving.

❀ In a small bowl, whisk together the olive oil, lime juice, paprika, salt, and pepper. Place the monkfish pieces in a shallow nonaluminum dish and spoon the olive oil mixture over the top. Turn over the fish to coat. Cover and refrigerate for 45 minutes. Remove from the refrigerator 15 minutes before grilling.

❀ Prepare a hot fire for direct-heat cooking in a grill (see page 10). Position the grill rack 4–6 inches (10–15 cm) above the fire.

❀ If the monkfish is in large pieces, place them directly on the rack. If the monkfish is in small pieces, place them in 1 or more lightly oiled hinged grill baskets. Cook, turning once, until the fish is opaque throughout and firm to the touch, 4–5 minutes on each side.

❀ Transfer the fish fillets to a warmed platter. Pass the sauce at the table.

NUTRITIONAL ANALYSIS PER SERVING: Calories 424 (Kilojoules 1,781); Protein 31 g; Carbohydrates 4 g; Total Fat 31 g; Saturated Fat 5 g; Cholesterol 71 mg; Sodium 509 mg; Dietary Fiber 0 g

Grilled Shrimp and Sausage with Red Rice

PREP TIME: 30 MINUTES, PLUS
3½ HOURS FOR MARINATING

COOKING TIME: 35 MINUTES,
PLUS PREPARING FIRE

INGREDIENTS

½ cup (6 oz/185 g) apricot preserves

2 tablespoons olive oil

2 teaspoons lemon juice

2 teaspoons Dijon mustard

16 large shrimp (prawns), peeled
and deveined

2 large red bell peppers (capsicums),
halved lengthwise, stemmed, and
seeded

1⅓ cups (10 oz/315 g) long-grain
white rice

2⅔ cups (21 fl oz/660 ml) water

2 tablespoons unsalted butter

4 green (spring) onions, white parts
and tender green tops chopped
separately

2 teaspoons chili powder

½ teaspoon salt

¼ cup (2 fl oz/60 ml) chicken broth

½ cup (4 fl oz/125 ml) dry white wine

4 sweet Italian sausages, about ¾ lb
(375 g) total weight

1 tablespoon chopped fresh parsley

SERVES 4

❀ In a saucepan over medium heat, combine the preserves, oil, lemon juice, and mustard. Bring to a boil, pour into a nonaluminum bowl, and let cool. Add the shrimp, cover, and refrigerate for 3 hours. Remove from the refrigerator 30 minutes before grilling.

❀ Meanwhile, preheat a broiler (griller). Place the peppers, cut sides down, on a baking sheet. Broil (grill) until the skins blacken and blister. Remove from the broiler, drape with foil, and let cool for 10 minutes, then peel away the skins. Chop the peppers.

❀ In a saucepan over medium-high heat, combine the rice and water. Bring to a boil, reduce the heat to low, cover, and cook until the rice is tender and the water is absorbed, about 18 minutes. Keep hot.

❀ Meanwhile, in a saucepan over medium-low heat, melt the butter. Add the white parts of the green onions and sauté until slightly softened, about 2 minutes. Stir in the chopped peppers, chili powder, salt, and broth. Cover and cook until the peppers are soft, 3–4 minutes. Transfer to a food processor and blend until smooth. Return to the pan.

❀ Prepare a hot fire for direct-heat cooking in a grill (see page 10). Position the grill rack 4–6 inches (10–15 cm) above the fire.

❀ In a frying pan just big enough to hold the sausages in a single layer, bring the wine to a boil over high heat. Reduce the heat to medium, add the sausages, prick in several places with a fork, and cook, turning once, for 4 minutes total. Transfer the sausages to the grill rack. Cover the grill and open the vents halfway. Cook, turning once, until cooked through, about 5 minutes total.

❀ Meanwhile, bend each shrimp almost in half and insert a metal skewer just above the tail so that it passes through the body twice. Grill, turning once, until cooked through, 3–4 minutes on each side.

❀ Slice the sausages, add to the red pepper purée, and place over medium-low heat. Stir briefly, add the hot rice, and mix thoroughly. Toss in the shrimp and the reserved green onion tops. Transfer to a warmed serving bowl, sprinkle with the parsley, and serve.

NUTRITIONAL ANALYSIS PER SERVING: Calories 709 (Kilojoules 2,978); Protein 26 g; Carbohydrates 83 g; Total Fat 30 g; Saturated Fat 10 g; Cholesterol 125 mg; Sodium 1,084 mg; Dietary Fiber 3 g

Pork Satay with Bell Pepper

PREP TIME: 15 MINUTES,
PLUS 2½ HOURS FOR
MARINATING

COOKING TIME: 10 MINUTES,
PLUS PREPARING FIRE

INGREDIENTS

1 clove garlic

1 shallot

¼ cup (1¼ oz/37 g) dry-roasted
peanuts

2 tablespoons ground coriander

1 tablespoon brown sugar

1 teaspoon salt

¼ teaspoon ground black pepper

⅛ teaspoon cayenne pepper

¼ cup (2 fl oz/60 ml) soy sauce

3 tablespoons lemon juice

1½ lb (750 g) boneless lean pork loin,
cut into 1-inch (2.5-cm) cubes

1 red bell pepper (capsicum), seeded
and cut into 1-inch (2.5-cm)
squares

1 green bell pepper (capsicum),
seeded and cut into 1-inch (2.5-cm)
squares

A heavy dose of coriander flavors this satay, giving the taste buds a real rush. Accompany these peanutty morsels with mashed sweet potatoes or saffron-scented couscous.

SERVES 4

❀ Turn on a food processor, drop the garlic clove and then the shallot through the feed tube, and process until minced. Add the peanuts, coriander, brown sugar, salt, black pepper, cayenne pepper, soy sauce, and lemon juice. Process until smooth. Transfer the mixture to a non-aluminum bowl and stir in the pork, coating evenly. Cover and refrigerate for at least 2 hours or for up to 6 hours. Remove from the refrigerator 30 minutes before grilling.

❀ Prepare a hot fire for direct-heat cooking in a grill (see page 10). Position the grill rack 4–6 inches (10–15 cm) above the fire.

❀ Meanwhile, bring a saucepan three-fourths full of salted water to a boil. Add the bell peppers and parboil for 3 minutes. Drain, rinse under cold running water, and drain again.

❀ Remove the pork from the marinade and divide into 4 equal portions. Thread the pork onto 4 metal skewers, alternating them with the pepper squares.

❀ Place the skewers on the rack. Cook, turning frequently, until nicely browned and the pork is no longer pink when a cube is cut into with a knife, 8–10 minutes.

❀ Transfer to warmed individual plates and serve immediately.

NUTRITIONAL ANALYSIS PER SERVING: Calories 321 (Kilojoules 1,348); Protein 39 g; Carbohydrates 7 g; Total Fat 15 g; Saturated Fat 5 g; Cholesterol 101 mg; Sodium 909 mg; Dietary Fiber 1 g

Leg of Lamb with Peppery Mint Jelly

PREP TIME: 15 MINUTES,
PLUS 2½ HOURS FOR
MARINATING

COOKING TIME: 1¼ HOURS,
PLUS PREPARING FIRE

INGREDIENTS

1 shank-end or sirloin half partial
bone-in leg of lamb, about 4 lb
(2 kg) *(see note)*

2 cloves garlic

½ cup (4 oz/125 g) Dijon mustard

2 tablespoons olive oil

2 tablespoons soy sauce

½ teaspoon chopped fresh rosemary
or thyme

½ teaspoon ground ginger

PEPPERY MINT JELLY

1 jar (12 oz/375 g) apple-mint jelly

¼ cup (3 oz/90 g) jalapeño jelly

1 tablespoon white wine vinegar

¼ cup (⅓ oz/10 g) chopped fresh
mint

PREP TIP: Lamb freezes well, so it is
sometimes more economical to pur-
chase a whole lamb leg weighing
about 8 pounds (4 kg), have the
butcher cut it in half, and then
freeze half for a future meal.

Nothing is more elegant than a leg of lamb served with mint jelly, and nothing is more delectable than a leg of lamb cooked on the grill. When choosing a bone-in leg of lamb for the grill, select a one-half or three-quarter leg weighing no more than 4 pounds (2 kg). This will keep the cooking time down to under 1½ hours.

SERVES 4–6

❊ Using the tip of a sharp knife, poke holes about ⅛ inch (3 mm) deep in the surface of the lamb. Sliver 1 of the garlic cloves and insert the slivers into the holes.

❊ Smash the remaining garlic clove with the side of a heavy knife and place in a small bowl. With the back of a spoon, mash the garlic to a coarse paste. Add the mustard, olive oil, soy sauce, rosemary or thyme, and ginger and mix well. Spread the mixture over the lamb, coating evenly, and place in a nonaluminum dish. Refrigerate, uncovered, for 2 hours. Remove from the refrigerator 30 minutes before cooking.

❊ Prepare a hot fire for indirect-heat cooking in a covered grill (see page 11). Position the grill rack 4–6 inches (10–15 cm) above the fire.

❊ Place the lamb on the rack over the drip pan. Cover the grill and position the vents three-quarters open. Cook until an instant-read ther-mometer inserted into the thickest part of the leg away from the bone registers 140°F (60°C) for medium-rare, about 1¼ hours, adding more coals as necessary after the first 45 minutes of cooking to maintain a constant temperature.

❊ Meanwhile, make the jelly: In a bowl, whisk together the apple-mint and jalapeño jellies and the wine vinegar until smooth. Whisk in the mint. Store tightly covered in the refrigerator until serving.

❊ When the lamb is done, transfer to a cutting board, tent loosely with aluminum foil, and let stand for about 15 minutes.

❊ Carve the meat across the grain into slices about ¼ inch (6 mm) thick, arrange on a warmed platter, and serve immediately. Pass the mint jelly at the table.

NUTRITIONAL ANALYSIS PER SERVING: Calories 794 (Kilojoules 3,335); Protein 57 g; Carbohydrates 62 g; Total Fat 32 g; Saturated Fat 12 g; Cholesterol 193 mg; Sodium 1,125 mg; Dietary Fiber 1 g

Porterhouse Steak with Sauce Rouille

PREP TIME: 20 MINUTES, PLUS
1 HOUR FOR MARINATING

COOKING TIME: 25 MINUTES,
PLUS PREPARING FIRE

INGREDIENTS

1 porterhouse steak, 2½–3 lb
(1.25–1.5 kg) and about 2 inches
(5 cm) thick

1 clove garlic, minced

1 teaspoon anchovy paste

2 teaspoons olive oil

¼ teaspoon ground pepper

SAUCE ROUILLE

1 russet potato, about 5 oz (155 g),
peeled and chopped

½ cup (4 fl oz/125 ml) chicken broth

1 small red bell pepper (capsicum),
seeded and chopped

3 cloves garlic

3 bottled hot cherry peppers,
drained and stems removed

1 jar (2 oz/60 g) chopped pimiento
pepper, drained

¼ teaspoon chopped fresh thyme

¼ teaspoon red wine vinegar

dash of hot-pepper sauce

about 5 tablespoons (2½ fl oz/75 ml)
olive oil

salt and ground pepper to taste

PREP TIP: If there's a long strip at one
end of your steak, secure it to the rest
of the meat with soaked toothpicks.

The best steaks for grilling are cut from the tender short loin:
porterhouse, T-bone, club, and shell or New York strip. Here,
a classic porterhouse is paired with a red pepper sauce.

SERVES 6

❀ Trim the fat from the edges of the steak, leaving a layer ¼ inch (6 mm)
thick, then slash the layer of fat at 1-inch (2.5-cm) intervals.

❀ In a small bowl, using the back of a spoon, mash together the garlic,
anchovy paste, olive oil, and pepper until smooth. Rub into both sides of
the steak. Cover and let stand at cool room temperature for 1 hour.

❀ Meanwhile, make the sauce: In a saucepan over medium-low heat,
combine the potato and chicken broth. Bring to a simmer and cook,
uncovered, until barely tender, about 10 minutes. Add the bell pepper
and cook until heated through, about 3 minutes longer. Drain, reserving
the broth. You should have 2–3 tablespoons.

❀ In a food processor, with the motor running, drop the garlic cloves
through the feed tube and process until chopped. Add the cherry peppers, pimientos, potato and bell pepper, thyme, vinegar, and hot-pepper
sauce. Process until smooth. With the motor running, slowly add the
oil, 1 tablespoon at a time, and process until the mixture thickens. Transfer
to a bowl and whisk in the reserved chicken broth. Season with salt and
pepper. Cover and refrigerate until serving.

❀ Prepare a hot fire for direct-heat cooking in a grill (see page 10).
Position the grill rack 4–6 inches (10–15 cm) above the fire.

❀ Place the steak on the rack and sear, turning once, until nicely
browned, about 1 minute on each side. Using long-handled tongs to hold
the meat, sear the edges. Then grill over a medium-hot fire (move the
steak to the edge of the coals or raise the grill rack), turning once, until
done to your liking, 16–20 minutes total for medium-rare. Transfer to a
cutting board and cover loosely with aluminum foil. Let stand for 5 minutes.

❀ Cut the meat from the bone, then slice the meat across the grain and
serve on a warmed platter. Pass the sauce at the table.

NUTRITIONAL ANALYSIS PER SERVING: Calories 500 (Kilojoules 2,100); Protein 30 g;
Carbohydrates 6 g; Total Fat 39 g; Saturated Fat 12 g; Cholesterol 97 mg; Sodium 263 mg;
Dietary Fiber 1 g

Chilied Flank Steak

PREP TIME: 10 MINUTES,
  PLUS 24 HOURS FOR
  MARINATING

COOKING TIME: 10 MINUTES,
  PLUS PREPARING FIRE

INGREDIENTS

1 flank steak, about 1½ lb (750 g)

⅓ cup (3 fl oz/80 ml) regular or spicy vegetable juice cocktail such as V-8 juice or Snappy Tom

⅓ cup (3 fl oz/80 ml) soy sauce

¼ cup (2 fl oz/60 ml) safflower oil

⅓ cup (2½ oz/75 g) firmly packed dark brown sugar

2 cloves garlic, minced

1 tablespoon chili powder

⅛ teaspoon ground cumin

Flank steak, a flavorful but not-so-tender cut, benefits from an overnight stint in a marinade. Scoring the flank steak helps keep it from shrinking too much as it cooks. Top round, often sold as London broil, or skirt steak can be substituted for the flank steak.

SERVES 4

❀ Using a sharp knife, score the flank steak on both sides, cutting about ⅛ inch (3 mm) deep and forming a diamond pattern.

❀ In a bowl, whisk together the vegetable juice cocktail, soy sauce, safflower oil, brown sugar, garlic, chili powder, and cumin. Pour half of the marinade into a shallow nonaluminum dish. Place the steak in the dish and pour the remaining marinade over the top. Cover and refrigerate for 24 hours. Remove from the refrigerator 30 minutes before grilling.

❀ Prepare a hot fire for direct-heat cooking in a grill (see page 10). Position the grill rack 4–6 inches (10–15 cm) above the fire.

❀ Remove the steak from the marinade and set aside. Pour the marinade into a small saucepan and bring to a boil over medium heat. Boil for 1 minute, remove from the heat, and strain through a sieve into a bowl. Cover and keep warm until serving.

❀ Place the steak on the rack. Cook, turning once, until done to your liking, about 4 minutes on each side for medium-rare. Transfer to a cutting board and cover loosely with aluminum foil. Let rest for 5 minutes.

❀ Carve the steak on the diagonal across the grain into slices about ¼ inch (6 mm) thick. Arrange on a warmed platter or individual plates. Pass the reserved marinade at the table.

NUTRITIONAL ANALYSIS PER SERVING: Calories 503 (Kilojoules 2,113); Protein 36 g; Carbohydrates 22 g; Total Fat 30 g; Saturated Fat 8 g; Cholesterol 87 mg; Sodium 1,551 mg; Dietary Fiber 1 g

Asian Skewered Lamb

PREP TIME: 20 MINUTES,
PLUS 2½ HOURS FOR
MARINATING

COOKING TIME: 12 MINUTES,
PLUS PREPARING FIRE

INGREDIENTS

1 cup (8 oz/250 g) plain yogurt

1 shallot, minced

1 tablespoon minced lemongrass
or 1½ teaspoons lemon zest

1 tablespoon soy sauce

2 teaspoons five-spice powder

1 teaspoon Asian sesame oil

2 lb (1 kg) boneless lamb from the
leg, cut into 1¼-inch (3-cm)
cubes (20 cubes)

8 small white onions, each about
1 inch (2.5 cm) in diameter

3 teaspoons olive oil

½ teaspoon curry powder

8 cherry tomatoes

1 teaspoon chopped fresh basil

A marinade containing lemongrass and five-spice powder (a commercial blend usually consisting of cinnamon, star anise, fennel seeds, Sichuan peppercorns, and cloves) gives these kabobs an exceptional flavor. Serve them with rice pilaf studded with toasted pine nuts.

SERVES 4

❋ In a large nonaluminum bowl, stir together the yogurt, shallot, lemongrass or lemon zest, soy sauce, five-spice powder, and sesame oil. Mix well. Stir in the lamb cubes, cover, and refrigerate for 2 hours. Remove from the refrigerator 30 minutes before grilling.

❋ Meanwhile, peel the onions, then cut a shallow cross in the root end of each onion. Bring a saucepan three-fourths full of water to a boil, add the onions, and boil for 3 minutes. Drain and rinse under running cold water. Pat dry with paper towels and place in a small bowl. Add 2 teaspoons of the olive oil and the curry powder. Mix well.

❋ Place the tomatoes in another bowl and add the remaining 1 teaspoon olive oil and the basil. Mix well.

❋ Prepare a hot fire for direct-heat cooking in a grill (see page 10). Position the rack 4–6 inches (10–15 cm) above the fire.

❋ Divide the meat into 4 equal portions; you should have 5 pieces per serving. Onto each of 4 metal skewers, thread the ingredients in the following order: lamb, onion, lamb, tomato, lamb, onion, lamb, tomato, lamb.

❋ Place the skewers on the rack. Cook, turning once, until nicely browned and done to your liking, 5–6 minutes on each side for medium-rare.

❋ Transfer the skewers to individual plates and serve hot.

NUTRITIONAL ANALYSIS PER SERVING: Calories 532 (Kilojoules 2,234); Protein 47 g; Carbohydrates 9 g; Total Fat 33 g; Saturated Fat 13 g; Cholesterol 160 mg; Sodium 413 mg; Dietary Fiber 1 g

Pork Chops with Green Chile and Pecan Stuffing

Double-thick pork chops are excellent when grilled, and these chops, filled with poblano chile and pecans, are irresistible.

PREP TIME: 30 MINUTES, PLUS
2¼ HOURS FOR MARINATING

COOKING TIME: 30 MINUTES

INGREDIENTS

4 double-thick pork chops

2 teaspoons Hungarian sweet paprika

1 teaspoon salt

½ teaspoon ground pepper

1 small poblano chile, about 2½ oz (75 g)

3 tablespoons unsalted butter

1 small yellow onion, chopped

1 cup (2 oz/60 g) dried bread cubes (¼-inch/6-mm cubes)

¼ cup (1 oz/30 g) chopped pecans

¼ cup (2 fl oz/60 ml) chicken broth

2 teaspoons olive oil

PREP TIP: If you can't find poblano chiles at your market, use 4 teaspoons chopped canned mild green chiles.

SERVES 4

❁ Place each chop on a cutting board and, using a small, sharp knife, cut a horizontal slit in the middle of the side, extending it about halfway along the length of the chop. Then, pressing down on the top of the chop, work the knife back and forth into the meat to form a pocket. Take care not to cut through the sides, top, or bottom. Alternatively, ask your butcher to cut the pockets. Sprinkle the chops inside and out with the paprika, salt, and pepper, place in a shallow dish, cover, and refrigerate for at least 2 hours or for up to 6. Remove from the refrigerator 15 minutes before stuffing.

❁ Meanwhile, preheat a broiler (griller). Place the chile on a baking sheet and broil (grill), turning as necessary, until the skin blackens and blisters. Remove from the broiler and drape loosely with aluminum foil. Let cool for 10 minutes, then peel away the skin. Remove the stem and seeds and chop finely. You should have about 4 teaspoons.

❁ In a saucepan over medium-low heat, melt the butter. Add the onion, cover, and cook, stirring occasionally, until softened, about 5 minutes. Stir in the poblano chile, bread cubes, and pecans, mixing well. Sprinkle the chicken broth over the mixture and stir again. Remove from the heat.

❁ Prepare a hot fire for direct-heat cooking in a covered grill (see page 10). Position the grill rack 4–6 inches (10–15 cm) above the fire. Soak 8 wooden toothpicks in water for at least 20 minutes.

❁ Meanwhile, using a teaspoon, stuff the chops with the bread cube mixture, dividing it evenly. Drain the toothpicks and use them to secure the openings closed. Brush each chop on both sides with ½ teaspoon oil.

❁ Place the chops on the rack and sear on each side for 1 minute. Then, holding the meat with long-handled tongs, sear the edges of the chops. Cover the grill and open the vents all the way. Cook, turning once, until an instant-read thermometer inserted into the thickest part of a chop away from the bone registers 160°F (71°C), about 25 minutes.

❁ Transfer to warmed individual plates, remove the toothpicks, and serve.

NUTRITIONAL ANALYSIS PER SERVING: Calories 677 (Kilojoules 2,843); Protein 34 g; Carbohydrates 16 g; Total Fat 53 g; Saturated Fat 19 g; Cholesterol 147 mg; Sodium 858 mg; Dietary Fiber 2 g

Baby Back Ribs with Peach Sauce

PREP TIME: 25 MINUTES, PLUS
24 HOURS FOR MARINATING

COOKING TIME: 1 HOUR,
PLUS PREPARING FIRE

INGREDIENTS

3 lb (1.5 kg) baby back ribs

2 lemons, halved

1 teaspoon ground pepper

½ teaspoon salt

PEACH SAUCE

1 cup (12 oz/375 g) peach preserves

1 yellow onion, finely chopped

¼ cup (2 oz/60 g) firmly packed
brown sugar

¼ cup (2 fl oz/60 ml) Worcestershire
sauce

¼ cup (2 fl oz/60 ml) cider vinegar

1 tablespoon ketchup

1 teaspoon dry mustard

1 teaspoon Hungarian sweet paprika

¼ teaspoon hot-pepper sauce

Nearly every barbecue cook has a favorite rub or sauce for pork ribs, along with a preferred technique. Some cooks like to parboil the ribs before saucing and finishing them on the grill. In this recipe, however, the ribs are cooked completely on the grill. For a bit of added color, you can garnish the ribs with sliced peaches.

SERVES 4

❀ Rub the ribs thoroughly with the lemon halves. Then rub them with the pepper and salt. Place in a shallow nonaluminum dish, cover, and refrigerate for 24 hours. Remove from the refrigerator 30 minutes before grilling.

❀ Meanwhile, make the peach sauce: In a saucepan over medium-low heat, combine the peach preserves, onion, brown sugar, Worcestershire sauce, vinegar, ketchup, dry mustard, paprika, and hot-pepper sauce. Bring to a boil, stirring occasionally to dissolve the sugar, then reduce the heat to medium-low and simmer, uncovered, until slightly thickened, about 10 minutes. Remove from the heat and let cool. Pour about ⅓ cup (3 fl oz/80 ml) of the sauce into a small bowl and reserve for basting.

❀ Prepare a hot fire for indirect-heat cooking in a covered grill (see page 11). Position the grill rack 4–6 inches (10–15 cm) above the fire.

❀ Place the ribs on the rack directly over the drip pan (you may require 2 pans). Cover the grill and open the vents halfway. Cook until tender, about 1 hour. (Charcoal grill users will need to add more partially lit coals after 40 minutes to maintain a constant temperature.) When the ribs are tender, move them over the direct heat and continue to grill, uncovered, turning once and basting with some of the peach sauce, until crisp on both sides, about 4 minutes longer.

❀ Cut the ribs into sections and place on a platter. Pour the remaining peach sauce into a bowl and pass at the table.

NUTRITIONAL ANALYSIS PER SERVING: Calories 912 (Kilojoules 3,830); Protein 42 g; Carbohydrates 78 g; Total Fat 49 g; Saturated Fat 18 g; Cholesterol 194 mg; Sodium 715 mg; Dietary Fiber 2 g

Asparagus with Parmesan Cheese

PREP TIME: 10 MINUTES,
   PLUS 30 MINUTES FOR
   MARINATING

COOKING TIME: 20 MINUTES,
   PLUS PREPARING FIRE

INGREDIENTS

1½ lb (750 g) asparagus

¼ cup (2 fl oz/60 ml) olive oil

1 green (spring) onion, minced

1 tablespoon fresh tarragon leaves

2 teaspoons chopped fresh parsley

¼ cup (1 oz/30 g) grated Parmesan cheese

PREP TIP: To keep asparagus fresh until ready to cook, stand the spears upright in a glass that contains about 1 inch (2.5 cm) of water and cover them with a plastic bag.

Fat spears of asparagus are the best choice for grilling. They're easier to handle and less likely to fall through the grill rack.

SERVES 4

❀ Snap the tough stem ends off the asparagus spears. Using a vegetable peeler and starting about 2 inches (5 cm) below the tip, peel off the thick outer skin. Place the stalks in a shallow nonaluminum dish.

❀ In a small bowl, stir together the olive oil, green onion, tarragon, and parsley. Pour over the asparagus. Toss to coat. Cover and let stand at room temperature for 30 minutes.

❀ Prepare a medium-hot fire for direct-heat cooking in a grill (see page 10). Position the grill rack 4–6 inches (10–15 cm) above the fire.

❀ Place the asparagus on the rack. Cook, turning once, until lightly browned, about 8 minutes total. Then continue to cook, turning several times (use the outer edges of the grill rack if the spears begin to burn), until crisp-tender, about 10 minutes longer. Transfer to a serving dish and immediately sprinkle with the Parmesan cheese. Serve at once.

NUTRITIONAL ANALYSIS PER SERVING: Calories 113 (Kilojoules 475); Protein 6 g; Carbohydrates 5 g; Total Fat 9 g; Saturated Fat 2 g; Cholesterol 4 mg; Sodium 96 mg; Dietary Fiber 1 g

South Fork Corn Salad

PREP TIME: 20 MINUTES, PLUS
1 HOUR FOR CHILLING

COOKING TIME: 3 MINUTES

INGREDIENTS

6 large ears of corn, husks and silk
removed

12 cherry tomatoes, or 1 large
tomato, chopped

1 large green bell pepper (capsicum),
seeded and chopped

1 celery stalk, chopped

1 small red (Spanish) onion, chopped

1 small jalapeño chile, seeded and
minced

½ cup (4 fl oz/125 ml) mayonnaise

¼ cup (2 oz/60 g) plain yogurt

¼ cup (2 fl oz/60 ml) chicken broth

2 tablespoons red wine vinegar

salt and ground pepper to taste

2 teaspoons chopped fresh cilantro
(fresh coriander)

2 teaspoons chopped fresh flat-leaf
(Italian) parsley

COOKING TIP: If you can't get fresh-
picked corn from your farmers'
market, you can salvage less-than-
stellar ears. Cook the corn in equal
amounts of milk and water to which
you have added 1 teaspoon sugar to
help bring back some of its original
sweetness.

This salad is a popular one at barbecues on what's known as the
South Fork of New York's Long Island. Serve it in August, when
corn and tomatoes are at their seasonal best. To turn this salad
into a light main course, add 2 cups (12 oz/375 g) diced cooked
chicken or turkey breast and serve on lettuce leaves.

SERVES 6

❀ Bring a large saucepan three-fourths full of water to a boil. Add the
corn and boil until just slightly cooked, about 3 minutes. Drain, rinse
under running cold water, and pat dry. Hold each corn cob by its pointed
end, steadying the stalk end on a cutting board. Using a sharp knife, cut
down along the corn cob to strip off the kernels, turning it with each cut.
In a bowl, combine the corn kernels with the tomatoes, bell pepper, celery,
onion, and jalapeño chile, tossing to mix well.

❀ In a bowl, whisk together the mayonnaise and yogurt until smooth.
Whisk in the chicken broth and vinegar. Pour over the corn mixture.
Toss well and season with salt and pepper. Cover and refrigerate for at
least 1 hour or for up to 3 hours.

❀ Remove from the refrigerator, transfer to a serving bowl, sprinkle
with the cilantro and parsley, and serve.

NUTRITIONAL ANALYSIS PER SERVING: Calories 316 (Kilojoules 1,327); Protein 7 g;
Carbohydrates 41 g; Total Fat 17 g; Saturated Fat 3 g; Cholesterol 11 mg; Sodium 192 mg;
Dietary Fiber 7 g

Grilled Summer Squash with Green Sauce

PREP TIME: 15 MINUTES,
PLUS 30 MINUTES FOR
MARINATING

COOKING TIME: 10 MINUTES,
PLUS PREPARING FIRE

INGREDIENTS

GREEN SAUCE

½ cup (4 fl oz/125 ml) olive oil

¼ cup (2 fl oz/60 ml) lemon juice

1 shallot, chopped

2 teaspoons capers

2 anchovy fillets in olive oil

½ teaspoon ground white pepper

½ cup (¾ oz/20 g) coarsely chopped
   fresh flat-leaf (Italian) parsley

½ cup (¾ oz/20 g) finely chopped
   fresh flat-leaf (Italian) parsley

¼ cup (⅓ oz/10 g) chopped fresh
   basil

4 or 5 small zucchini (courgettes) or
   yellow summer squash, about 1 lb
   (500 g) total weight, cut lengthwise
   into slices ¼ inch (6 mm) thick

4 cloves garlic, minced

6 tablespoons (3 fl oz/90 ml) olive oil

1 tablespoon chopped fresh thyme

½ teaspoon salt

¼ teaspoon ground black pepper

Zucchini is one of the most popular vegetables for grilling. It's easy to prepare, cooks quickly, and is delicious, particularly when served with this tasty green sauce.

SERVES 4

❁ To make the green sauce, in a food processor, combine the olive oil, lemon juice, shallot, capers, anchovies, white pepper, and the coarsely chopped parsley. Process until smooth. Transfer to a bowl and stir in the finely chopped parsley and the basil. Cover and refrigerate until ready to serve.

❁ Place the zucchini in a large, shallow nonaluminum dish. In a small bowl, mash together the garlic and 2 tablespoons of the olive oil with the back of a spoon until smooth. Whisk in the remaining 4 tablespoons (2 fl oz/60 ml) oil, the thyme, salt, and black pepper. Pour over the zucchini. Cover and let stand at room temperature for 30 minutes.

❁ Prepare a hot fire for direct-heat cooking in a grill (see page 10). Position the grill rack 4–6 inches (10–15 cm) above the fire.

❁ Place the zucchini on the rack. Cook, turning once, until just tender, 4–5 minutes on each side.

❁ Transfer to a serving dish and spoon the green sauce evenly over the top. Serve immediately.

NUTRITIONAL ANALYSIS PER SERVING: Calories 454 (Kilojoules 1,907); Protein 3 g; Carbohydrates 7 g; Total Fat 48 g; Saturated Fat 6 g; Cholesterol 1 mg; Sodium 438 mg; Dietary Fiber 1 g

Mushroom and Spinach Salad

PREP TIME: 15 MINUTES,
PLUS 20 MINUTES FOR
MARINATING

COOKING TIME: 15 MINUTES,
PLUS PREPARING FIRE

INGREDIENTS

1 lb (500 g) fresh small portobello mushrooms, brushed clean and stems removed

¼ cup (2 fl oz/60 ml) safflower oil

1 teaspoon chopped fresh sage

½ teaspoon ground pepper

¼ cup (1 oz/30 g) walnuts

10 oz (315 g) spinach, stems removed

2 tablespoons walnut oil

3 teaspoons lemon juice

2 teaspoons red wine vinegar

Hinged grill baskets make grilling just about anything possible—even spinach. This unusual salad is best served the moment the ingredients come off the grill. Do not substitute another oil for the walnut oil; it is an essential component of the finished dish. Cremini, porcini, or shiitakes can be used in place of the portobellos.

SERVES 4

❋ In a bowl, lightly toss the mushrooms with the safflower oil, sage, and pepper. Cover and let stand at room temperature for 20 minutes.

❋ Meanwhile, preheat an oven to 350°F (180°C). Spread the walnuts on a baking sheet and toast until they are lightly browned and fragrant, 5–7 minutes. Remove from the oven, chop coarsely, and set aside.

❋ Prepare a hot fire for direct-heat cooking in a grill (see page 10). Position the grill rack 4–6 inches (10–15 cm) above the fire.

❋ Place the mushrooms on the rack, gill side down. (If the mushrooms are quite small, put them in a lightly oiled hinged grill basket.) Cook until lightly browned, about 3 minutes. Turn and continue to cook until browned and just tender, about 4 minutes longer. Transfer to a plate.

❋ Arrange the spinach leaves over the bottom of a lightly oiled hinged grill basket. Close the basket and sprinkle each side with 1 tablespoon of the walnut oil, 1½ teaspoons of the lemon juice, and 1 teaspoon of the vinegar.

❋ Place the basket on the rack. Cook the spinach, turning once, just until slightly wilted, about 3 minutes on each side. Transfer to a serving bowl.

❋ Slice the mushrooms about ⅛ inch (3 mm) thick. Add to the spinach leaves along with the toasted walnuts. Toss to mix.

❋ Serve immediately.

NUTRITIONAL ANALYSIS PER SERVING: Calories 236 (Kilojoules 991); Protein 5 g; Carbohydrates 9 g; Total Fat 22 g; Saturated Fat 2 g; Cholesterol 0 mg; Sodium 46 mg; Dietary Fiber 3 g

Bourbon Baked Beans

PREP TIME: 20 MINUTES,
   PLUS 1 HOUR FOR SOAKING
   THE BEANS

COOKING TIME: 3½ HOURS

INGREDIENTS

2¼ cups (1 lb/500 g) dried Great
   Northern or other large white
   beans

1 clove garlic, lightly crushed

6 slices thick-cut bacon

1 large yellow onion, finely chopped

1½ cups (12 fl oz/375 ml) beef broth

½ cup (4 fl oz/125 ml) bourbon
   whiskey

5 tablespoons (2½ fl oz/75 ml)
   bottled chili sauce

¼ cup (2½ oz/75 g) molasses

2 teaspoons Worcestershire sauce

2 tablespoons dark brown sugar

1 tablespoon dry mustard

1 teaspoon curry powder

½ teaspoon ground pepper

¼ teaspoon Hungarian hot paprika

COOKING TIP: An old-fashioned clay
bean pot is ideal for baking beans.
The lid forms a better seal than one
on a conventional pot, so less liquid
is lost during cooking and the beans
stay moist. Also, clay does not conduct
heat as well as metal does, so the
beans cook more slowly and evenly.

Baked beans have a long history in the United States. Native Americans traditionally flavored them with chunks of bear fat and cooked them in a covered clay pot in a hole lined with hot rocks. In this version, bourbon, rather than bear fat, gives the finished beans their distinctive flavor.

SERVES 6

❀ Pick over the beans and discard any misshapen beans or stones. Rinse the beans and drain. Place in a large pot and add water to cover by 2 inches (5 cm). Bring to a boil and boil for 2 minutes. Remove from the heat, cover, and let stand for 1 hour. Drain.

❀ Preheat an oven to 300°F (150°C). Butter a bean pot or Dutch oven and rub with the garlic clove. Then mince the garlic and set aside.

❀ Chop 3 of the bacon slices. In a large pot over medium heat, sauté the chopped bacon until crisp, 3–4 minutes. Add the onion and sauté until just beginning to soften, about 1 minute. Add the reserved garlic and sauté until the onion and garlic are lightly browned, about 4 minutes longer. Stir in ½ cup (4 fl oz/125 ml) of the beef broth, the bourbon, chili sauce, molasses, Worcestershire sauce, brown sugar, mustard, curry powder, pepper, and paprika. Mix well, stir in the drained beans, and transfer to the prepared pot. Lay the remaining 3 slices bacon evenly over the top.

❀ Cover and bake for 2 hours. Reduce the oven temperature to 275°F (135°C) and continue to bake, adding the remaining 1 cup (8 fl oz/250 ml) broth as needed to keep the beans from drying out, until tender, about 1½ hours longer. Uncover and cut the bacon—which will have shrunk quite a bit—into pieces with scissors. Serve the beans hot.

NUTRITIONAL ANALYSIS PER SERVING: Calories 565 (Kilojoules 2,373); Protein 22 g; Carbohydrates 68 g; Total Fat 24 g; Saturated Fat 9 g; Cholesterol 28 mg; Sodium 699 mg; Dietary Fiber 31 g

Corn Bread with Chorizo

PREP TIME: 35 MINUTES

COOKING TIME: 1 HOUR, PLUS
15 MINUTES FOR COOLING

INGREDIENTS

1 teaspoon plus 2 tablespoons
olive oil

4 chorizo sausages, about 10 oz
(315 g) total weight, chopped

6 green (spring) onions, white parts
and tender green tops chopped
separately

1 red bell pepper (capsicum), seeded
and chopped

1 cup (5 oz/155 g) yellow cornmeal

⅓ cup (2 oz/60 g) all-purpose (plain)
flour

1 teaspoon baking powder

1 teaspoon sugar

½ teaspoon baking soda (bicarbonate
of soda)

½ teaspoon salt

2 eggs

¾ cup (6 oz/185 g) plain yogurt

½ cup (4 fl oz/125 ml) bottled
medium-hot, chunky-style salsa

⅔ cup (5 fl oz/160 ml) milk

¼ lb (125 g) Monterey jack cheese,
shredded

MAKE-AHEAD TIP: If you like, bake
the corn bread several hours in
advance, keep at room temperature,
and then reheat in a 350°F (180°C)
oven just before serving.

This flavor-laced corn bread is the perfect mate for many grilled foods, from brisket to ribs. The recipe calls for a bottled chunky-style tomato salsa, but if you have homemade salsa on hand, use it instead.

SERVES 8

❂ Preheat an oven to 350°F (180°C).

❂ In a 10-inch (25-cm) cast-iron or other ovenproof frying pan over medium-low heat, warm the 1 teaspoon olive oil until hot. Add the chorizo and sauté, stirring occasionally, until lightly browned and all the fat has been rendered, about 8 minutes. Using a slotted spoon, transfer the sausage to a plate.

❂ Pour off all but 1 tablespoon fat from the pan and return to medium-low heat. Add the white parts of the green onions and sauté until lightly browned, about 4 minutes. Return the chorizo to the pan and stir in the bell pepper. Cover and cook, stirring occasionally, until the pepper begins to soften, about 4 minutes. Uncover and remove from the heat.

❂ In a bowl, stir together the cornmeal, flour, baking powder, sugar, baking soda, and salt.

❂ In a large bowl, whisk together the eggs, yogurt, and the 2 tablespoons olive oil until smooth. Add the salsa and green onion tops and then stir in the cornmeal mixture in 3 batches, alternating with the milk and ending with the cornmeal. Stir in the cheese and the chorizo mixture. Immediately pour the batter into the frying pan (do not wipe out the pan) and smooth the top.

❂ Bake until golden and firm to the touch, about 40 minutes. Remove from the oven and let stand for at least 15 minutes before serving. Cut into wedges and serve directly from the pan.

NUTRITIONAL ANALYSIS PER SERVING: Calories 392 (Kilojoules 1,646); Protein 18 g; Carbohydrates 26 g; Total Fat 24 g; Saturated Fat 9 g; Cholesterol 103 mg; Sodium 1,001 mg; Dietary Fiber 2 g

Old-fashioned Potato Salad

PREP TIME: 35 MINUTES

COOKING TIME: 20 MINUTES

INGREDIENTS

2 lb (1 kg) boiling potatoes
  (about 4 potatoes)

½ cup (3 oz/90 g) chopped dill pickles

4 hard-boiled eggs, peeled and
  coarsely chopped

1 celery stalk, finely chopped

1 large clove garlic, minced

½ teaspoon salt

2 tablespoons lemon juice

2 teaspoons Dijon mustard

1 teaspoon Hungarian sweet paprika

⅛ teaspoon cayenne pepper

⅔ cup (5 fl oz/160 ml) mayonnaise

¼ cup (2 fl oz/60 ml) olive oil

salt and ground black pepper to
  taste

1 tablespoon chopped fresh flat-leaf
  (Italian) parsley

COOKING TIP: It is important not to overcook the potatoes. To test for doneness, insert a small, sharp knife into the center of a potato. The tip should encounter a slight resistance halfway through. The center will continue to cook as the potato cools.

When choosing potatoes for salad, opt for waxy boiling types such as Red Bliss or red or white new potatoes. They hold their shape better than baking potatoes.

SERVES 6

❀ In a saucepan, combine the potatoes with water to cover. Bring to a boil over high heat and boil until just barely tender, about 20 minutes. Drain, rinse under running cold water, and drain again. Let cool slightly.

❀ Peel the potatoes and cut in half lengthwise. Cut each half into slices about ¼ inch (6 mm) thick. In a large bowl, combine the potatoes, dill pickles, eggs, and celery.

❀ In a small bowl, mash together the garlic and salt with the back of a spoon to form a paste. Stir in the lemon juice, mustard, paprika, and cayenne. Whisk in the mayonnaise and olive oil. Pour over the potato mixture and toss gently to mix. Season with salt and pepper. Cover and refrigerate until needed. Remove from the refrigerator about 30 minutes before serving.

❀ Serve slightly chilled or at room temperature. Sprinkle with the parsley just before serving.

NUTRITIONAL ANALYSIS PER SERVING: Calories 435 (Kilojoules 1,827); Protein 7 g; Carbohydrates 30 g; Total Fat 32 g; Saturated Fat 5 g; Cholesterol 156 mg; Sodium 609 mg; Dietary Fiber 2 g

Ratatouille on the Grill

PREP TIME: 30 MINUTES, PLUS
ABOUT 45 MINUTES FOR
SOAKING AND MARINATING

COOKING TIME: 30 MINUTES,
PLUS PREPARING FIRE

INGREDIENTS

1 large Vidalia or other sweet onion,
    unpeeled

2 small eggplants (aubergines), about
    1 lb (500 g) total weight

salt to taste

1 large green bell pepper (capsicum)

1 large red bell pepper (capsicum)

2 firm but ripe tomatoes, halved
    crosswise

about ¼ cup (2 fl oz/60 ml) olive oil

2 yellow summer squashes, cut
    lengthwise into slices ¼ inch
    (6 mm) thick

1 clove garlic, minced

½ teaspoon chopped fresh thyme

½ teaspoon red pepper flakes

1 tablespoon chopped fresh dill, plus
    sprigs for garnish (optional)

COOKING TIP: If you're using a gas
grill, peel 2 onions and cut a shallow
cross in the root ends. Bring a
saucepan three-fourths full of water
to a boil, add the onions, parboil for
5 minutes, and drain. Brush with
olive oil, place on the grill rack,
cover, and cook, turning once, for
10 minutes on each side.

SERVES 4

❀ Soak the onion in cold water for about 30 minutes.

❀ Meanwhile, cut the eggplants lengthwise into slices ¼ inch (6 mm)
thick. Sprinkle with salt and place in a colander. Let stand, turning
once, for 30 minutes. Rinse under cold running water and pat dry with
paper towels.

❀ Prepare a hot fire for direct-heat cooking in a covered grill (see page 10).
Position the grill rack 4–6 inches (10–15 cm) above the fire.

❀ When the coals are covered with white ash, drain the onion and carefully place it directly in the hot coals, making sure it is well covered.
Cook until soft in the center when pierced with a sharp knife, about
30 minutes. Carefully remove from the coals and let cool.

❀ Meanwhile, brush the eggplant slices, whole peppers, and tomato
halves with about 2 teaspoons of the olive oil. Place the eggplant around
the edges of the rack and the peppers and the tomato halves, cut sides
down, in the center. Cover the grill and open the vents. Cook, turning
occasionally, until the eggplant and tomatoes are just tender and the
peppers are tender and well charred on all sides, about 10 minutes for
the tomatoes, 15 minutes for the eggplant, and 25 minutes for the peppers.
As the vegetables are ready, transfer them to a cutting board. Drape the
peppers with aluminum foil and let stand for about 10 minutes, then
peel away the skin. Remove the stems, seeds, and ribs, then cut lengthwise into strips ¼ inch (6 mm) wide. Cut each strip in half crosswise.

❀ Meanwhile, brush the squash slices with about ½ teaspoon oil. As the
other vegetables are removed from the rack, place the squash slices on
the rack. Cook, turning once, until tender, about 5 minutes on each side.

❀ Peel the onion and cut in half. Cut each half into slices ¼ inch (6 mm)
thick. Transfer to a large bowl. Coarsely chop the tomatoes and squash.
Cut the eggplant crosswise into narrow strips. Add to the onion along
with the pepper strips. Add 3 tablespoons olive oil, the garlic, thyme, and
red pepper flakes. Toss lightly to mix. Season with salt and toss again.

❀ Sprinkle with the chopped dill and garnish with dill sprigs, if desired.
Serve warm or at room temperature.

NUTRITIONAL ANALYSIS PER SERVING: Calories 228 (Kilojoules 958); Protein 4 g;
Carbohydrates 25 g; Total Fat 14 g; Saturated Fat 2 g; Cholesterol 0 mg; Sodium 22 mg;
Dietary Fiber 6 g

Stuffed Crookneck Squash

PREP TIME: 25 MINUTES

COOKING TIME: 30 MINUTES,
PLUS PREPARING FIRE

INGREDIENTS

4 crookneck squashes, about ½ lb
(250 g) each

¼ cup (1 oz/30 g) pine nuts

2 tablespoons unsalted butter

2 green (spring) onions, white parts
and tender green tops chopped
separately

1 small clove garlic, minced

¾ cup (4½ oz/140 g) diced cooked
chicken

⅓ cup (2 oz/60 g) chopped prosciutto

1 tablespoon curry powder

½ teaspoon salt

¼ teaspoon ground pepper

COOKING TIP: If the tops of the
squashes are not lightly browned,
slip them under a preheated broiler
(griller) for a minute or two before
serving.

Filled with a curry-flavored mixture of chopped squash, chicken,
and prosciutto, these stuffed squashes make a fine light meal
accompanied with crusty bread and a green salad.

SERVES 4

❀ Using a sharp knife, cut a thin, even slice off the entire length of each
squash. Then, using a paring knife or a vegetable peeler, peel the skin
from the slice and finely chop the flesh. Transfer to a bowl.

❀ Using the sharp knife, cut several slashes across the exposed flesh
of each squash. Then, with a teaspoon, gently scoop out the flesh from
the squashes, including the necks, leaving shells about ¹⁄₁₆ inch (2 mm)
thick. Be very careful not to puncture the skins. Finely chop the flesh
and add to the bowl.

❀ Bring a saucepan three-fourths full of salted water to a boil, add the
squash shells, and parboil for 30 seconds. Using tongs, carefully remove
and invert to drain.

❀ In a small, dry frying pan, toast the pine nuts, stirring often, until
lightly golden and fragrant, 2–3 minutes. Transfer to a plate.

❀ In a frying pan over medium-low heat, melt the butter. Add the white
parts of the green onions and sauté until beginning to soften, about
1 minute. Add the garlic and sauté until translucent, about 2 minutes
longer. Stir in the chopped squash and continue to cook, stirring frequently, until softened, about 5 minutes. Add the chicken, prosciutto,
curry powder, salt, pepper, and pine nuts. Mix well and remove from
the heat. Spoon the mixture into the squash shells, dividing it evenly.
Sprinkle evenly with the green onion tops.

❀ Prepare a hot fire for direct-heat cooking in a covered grill (see page 10).
Position the grill rack 4–6 inches (10–15 cm) above the fire.

❀ Place the squashes on the rack. Cover the grill and open the vents
halfway. Cook until lightly browned and the squashes are tender when
pierced with a knife tip, about 20 minutes. (If the squashes begin to
burn on the bottom, move them to the outer edges of the rack.)

❀ Transfer to individual plates and serve hot.

NUTRITIONAL ANALYSIS PER SERVING: Calories 234 (Kilojoules 983); Protein 18 g;
Carbohydrates 12 g; Total Fat 14 g; Saturated Fat 5 g; Cholesterol 55 mg; Sodium 584 mg;
Dietary Fiber 2 g

Corn on the Cob with Pepper Butter

PREP TIME: 35 MINUTES, PLUS
15 MINUTES FOR SOAKING

COOKING TIME: 15 MINUTES,
PLUS PREPARING FIRE

INGREDIENTS

1 small red bell pepper (capsicum)

2 tablespoons chicken broth, or as needed

¼ cup (2 oz/60 g) unsalted butter, at room temperature

salt and ground pepper to taste

8 ears of corn with husks intact

PREP TIP: When shopping for corn, look for ears with dark green husks and tassels that are brown on top but not too dry. Don't pull back the husks to check the kernels. The husks are nature's own freshness seal. Once they're gone, the corn will quickly age.

Nothing tastes better than plain grilled corn on the cob, except, perhaps, corn that has been rubbed with a pepper butter before grilling. Corn is always best if you cook it the day it is picked. If a few husks become detached from the ears while you are cleaning away the silk, don't worry. Simply tie them back into place, covering any exposed corn.

SERVES 4

❀ Preheat a broiler (griller). Cut the bell pepper in half lengthwise and remove the stem, seeds, and ribs. Place, cut sides down, on a baking sheet. Broil (grill) until the skin blackens and blisters. Remove from the broiler, drape the pepper loosely with aluminum foil, let cool for 10 minutes, then peel away the skin. Chop coarsely.

❀ In a food processor or blender, combine the bell pepper and 2 tablespoons chicken broth. Process until smooth, adding more broth if needed. The mixture should be quite thick. Transfer to a bowl and whisk in the butter until smooth. Season with salt and pepper.

❀ Carefully peel back the husks from the corn, but do not detach. Remove the silk. Using a sharp knife, carefully cut each cob from the stalk end without cutting into the husks. Rub each ear with about 1 tablespoon of the pepper butter. Replace the corn, re-form the husks around the ears, and tightly tie each in place at the top and middle with kitchen string. Place the ears in a sink or large pot, add cold water to cover, and let soak for 15 minutes before grilling.

❀ Prepare a medium-hot fire for direct-heat cooking in a covered grill (see page 10). Position the grill rack 4–6 inches (10–15 cm) above the fire.

❀ Place the corn on the rack. Cover the grill and open the vents all the way. Cook, turning frequently, until the husks are browned and crisp, about 15 minutes.

❀ Transfer the corn to a serving platter and remove the strings. Let diners unwrap their own corn.

NUTRITIONAL ANALYSIS PER SERVING: Calories 354 (Kilojoules 1,487); Protein 10 g; Carbohydrates 56 g; Total Fat 15 g; Saturated Fat 8 g; Cholesterol 31 mg; Sodium 77 mg; Dietary Fiber 9 g

Peach and Berry Shortcake

PREP TIME: 25 MINUTES, PLUS
2 HOURS FOR CHILLING

COOKING TIME: 20 MINUTES,
PLUS 1 HOUR FOR COOLING

INGREDIENTS

2 oz (60 g) blanched slivered
   almonds (about ½ cup)

1½ cups (12 oz/375 g) plus 2 tablespoons sugar

½ cup (4 oz/125 g) unsalted butter,
   at room temperature

4 eggs, separated

1½ teaspoons vanilla extract
   (essence)

1 cup (5 oz/155 g) all-purpose
   (plain) flour

1 tablespoon baking powder

½ cup (4 fl oz/125 ml) milk

2½ cups (20 fl oz/625 ml) heavy
   (double) cream

3 cups (1 lb/500 g) peeled peach
   slices (about 1¼ lb/625 g peaches)

¾ cup (3 oz/90 g) fresh or thawed
   frozen Marionberries or other
   varietal blackberries, raspberries,
   or sliced strawberries

PREP TIP: To peel a peach, dip it into
boiling water for 30 seconds, and then
plunge it into ice water. The skin will
slip off. To prevent freshly cut peach
slices from browning, immediately
dip them into 1 cup (8 fl oz/250 ml)
water mixed with the juice of ½ lemon.

SERVES 8

❊ Preheat an oven to 325°F (165°C). Lightly butter two 9-inch (23-cm)
round cake pans.

❊ In a food processor or blender, process the almonds with 2 tablespoons of the sugar until they resemble coarse meal.

❊ In a large bowl, using an electric mixer set on high speed, beat together
the butter and 6 tablespoons (3 oz/90 g) of the remaining sugar until
light and smooth, about 2 minutes. Add the egg yolks, one at a time,
beating well after each addition. Slowly beat in 1 teaspoon of the vanilla,
the flour, ground almonds, baking powder, milk, and ½ cup (4 fl oz/125 ml)
of the cream. Beat until smooth and thick. Divide evenly between the
prepared pans.

❊ In a large bowl, using an electric mixer fitted with clean beaters, beat
the egg whites on high speed until soft peaks form. Continue beating,
slowly adding 1 cup (8 oz/250 g) of the remaining sugar until stiff but
not dry. Dividing evenly, spoon the egg whites onto the batter in the
pans. Spread them evenly and smoothly over the tops, making sure the
batter is completely covered.

❊ Bake until the tops are golden and firm to the touch, about 20 minutes. Turn off the oven and leave the cakes in it with the oven door closed
for 25 minutes. Then transfer to a rack and let cool completely. If the
tops are very uneven, trim them with a sharp knife.

❊ Meanwhile, in a bowl, combine the peach slices and the remaining
2 tablespoons sugar and ½ teaspoon vanilla. Let stand for 30 minutes.

❊ Drain the peaches, then drain the berries, if needed. Run a knife
around the edge of each cake pan. Invert a cake layer onto a serving
plate and lift off the pan. The meringue layer will crumble a bit.

❊ In a large bowl, beat the remaining 2 cups (16 fl oz/500 ml) cream
until stiff peaks form. Spread half of the cream over the cake layer.
Arrange half of the peach slices and half of the berries on top. Invert
the second cake layer onto the fruit layer and press down gently. Cover
with the remaining whipped cream, peaches, and berries. Refrigerate
for 2–6 hours. Remove from the refrigerator 15 minutes before serving.

NUTRITIONAL ANALYSIS PER SERVING: Calories 710 (Kilojoules 2,982); Protein 9 g;
Carbohydrates 67 g; Total Fat 47 g; Saturated Fat 26 g; Cholesterol 244 mg; Sodium 263 mg;
Dietary Fiber 2 g

Strawberry-Raspberry Sherbet

PREP TIME: 20 MINUTES

INGREDIENTS

1 package (10 oz/315 g) frozen raspberries, thawed, drained, and juice reserved

about ¾ cup (6 fl oz/180 ml) water

4 cups (1 lb/500 g) fresh strawberries, stems removed

1 cup (8 oz/250 g) sugar

½ cup (4 fl oz/125 ml) heavy (double) cream

fresh raspberries, for garnish (optional)

PREP TIP: If you don't own an ice-cream maker, pour the sherbet mixture into a large metal bowl, cover, and place in the freezer until frozen 2 inches (5 cm) in from the sides, about 2 hours. Scrape the partially frozen mixture into a food processor and process just until smooth. Return to the bowl, cover, and return to the freezer. Repeat the freezing and processing two more times, then transfer the mixture to a 1½-qt (1½-l) container and allow it to freeze solid.

Frozen raspberries are the secret to this refreshing dessert. They both sweeten the sherbet and bring out the naturally robust flavor of the fresh strawberries.

MAKES ABOUT 5 CUPS (40 FL OZ/1.25 L); SERVES 6

❈ Measure the reserved raspberry juice; you should have about ¾ cup (6 fl oz/180 ml). Add water as needed to make 1½ cups (12 fl oz/375 ml) liquid.

❈ In a food processor, combine the raspberries, strawberries, sugar, and the 1½ cups (12 fl oz/375 ml) juice mixture. Process until smooth. Transfer to a large bowl.

❈ In another large bowl, using an electric mixer or a whisk, beat the cream until soft peaks form. Using a rubber spatula, fold the cream into the berry mixture.

❈ Transfer to an ice-cream maker and freeze according to the manufacturer's instructions.

❈ To serve, scoop into chilled bowls and garnish with fresh raspberries, if you like.

NUTRITIONAL ANALYSIS PER SERVING: Calories 285 (Kilojoules 1,197); Protein 1 g; Carbohydrates 56 g; Total Fat 8 g; Saturated Fat 5 g; Cholesterol 27 mg; Sodium 9 mg; Dietary Fiber 2 g

Lemon and Lime Tart

PREP TIME: 20 MINUTES,
   PLUS 1 HOUR FOR CHILLING
   DOUGH AND 30 MINUTES
   FOR COOLING CRUST

COOKING TIME: 1 HOUR

INGREDIENTS
TART SHELL
1¼ cups (6½ oz/200 g) all-purpose
   (plain) flour

¼ teaspoon salt

¼ teaspoon finely grated lemon zest

¼ cup (2 oz/60 g) chilled unsalted
   butter, cut into pieces

¼ cup (2 oz/60 g) chilled vegetable
   shortening, cut into pieces

2 tablespoons cold water

LEMON AND LIME FILLING
6 eggs

⅔ cup (5 oz/155 g) sugar

juice of 3 lemons

juice of 2 limes

1½ cups (12 fl oz/375 ml) heavy
   (double) cream

6 tablespoons (3 oz/90 g) unsalted
   butter, melted

PREP TIP: Bring lemons and limes
to room temperature and roll them
gently between your palms before
squeezing, and they will yield
more juice.

Tart, citrusy desserts are perfect after a barbecue dinner. If you like, use just lemon juice or lime juice, or even all orange juice. Don't worry if the top of the tart cracks during baking; you can either hide the damage with whipped cream or just ignore it. The first taste will make you forget any imperfections.

SERVES 8

❅ To make the tart shell, in a large bowl, stir together the flour, salt, and lemon zest. Add the butter and shortening and, using a pastry blender or 2 knives, cut them in until the mixture resembles coarse crumbs. Add the water, 1 tablespoon at a time, mixing gently with a fork or your fingertips until a soft dough forms. Do not overwork the dough. Gather into a ball, flatten into a disk, wrap in plastic wrap, and refrigerate for 1 hour.

❅ Preheat an oven to 400°F (200°C). On a lightly floured work surface, roll out the dough into a round 12 inches (30 cm) in diameter. Drape the dough over the rolling pin and carefully transfer it to a 10-inch (25-cm) tart pan with a removable bottom. Gently ease the pastry into the pan. Trim the pastry even with the pan rim. Line the pastry with aluminum foil and fill with dried beans or pie weights.

❅ Bake for 10 minutes. Remove the weights and foil and bake until firm and dry, about 5 minutes longer. Transfer to a rack to cool, about 30 minutes.

❅ Reduce the oven temperature to 325°F (165°C).

❅ To make the filling, in a large bowl, using an electric mixer set on high speed, beat together the eggs and sugar until light and lemon colored, 4–5 minutes. Beat in the lemon juice, lime juice, cream, and melted butter until fully incorporated. Pour into the tart shell.

❅ Bake until firm to the touch, about 45 minutes. Transfer to a rack and let cool completely, about 45 minutes. Serve at room temperature or slightly chilled.

NUTRITIONAL ANALYSIS PER SERVING: Calories 560 (Kilojoules 2,352); Protein 8 g; Carbohydrates 39 g; Total Fat 42 g; Saturated Fat 22 g; Cholesterol 259 mg; Sodium 138 mg; Dietary Fiber 1 g

Peanut Butter Pie with Mocha Crust

PREP TIME: 25 MINUTES,
    PLUS 1 HOUR FOR COOLING
    CRUST

COOKING TIME: 15 MINUTES,
    PLUS 2 HOURS FOR
    CHILLING

INGREDIENTS

MOCHA PIE SHELL

6 tablespoons (3 oz/90 g) unsalted
    butter, melted and cooled

1 teaspoon instant-coffee powder

1½ cups (6 oz/185 g) chocolate
    wafer crumbs (about 30 wafers)

¼ cup (1 oz/30 g) confectioners'
    (icing) sugar

PEANUT BUTTER FILLING

¼ lb (125 g) cream cheese, at room
    temperature

1½ cups (15 oz/470 g) smooth
    peanut butter

1 cup (4 oz/125 g) confectioners'
    (icing) sugar, sifted

½ cup (4 fl oz/125 ml) milk

2 teaspoons vanilla extract (essence)

2 cups (16 fl oz/500 ml) heavy
    (double) cream

1 oz (30 g) semisweet (plain) choco-
    late, at cool room temperature

Peanut butter pie appears on barbecue restaurant menus every-where from North Carolina to Texas to New York City. This version, although creamy and rich, has a light texture that appeals to kids of all ages.

SERVES 8

❀ Preheat an oven to 300°F (150°C). Butter a 9-inch (23-cm) pie pan.

❀ To make the pie shell, in a bowl, stir together the butter and coffee powder. Stir in the wafer crumbs and confectioners' sugar, mixing thoroughly. Transfer the crumb mixture to the prepared pie pan and press evenly over the bottom and sides.

❀ Bake until firm, about 15 minutes. Transfer to a rack and let cool completely, about 1 hour.

❀ To make the filling, in a large bowl, using an electric mixer set on high speed, beat together the cream cheese and peanut butter until smooth, about 3 minutes. Reduce the speed to low, add the confectioners' sugar, and beat until fully incorporated. Increase the speed to high and beat until fluffy, about 1 minute. Beat in the milk and vanilla until fully incorporated.

❀ In another large bowl, using an electric mixer fitted with clean beaters, beat the cream until stiff peaks form. Transfer 1 cup (8 fl oz/250 ml) of the whipped cream to a small bowl, cover, and refrigerate.

❀ Stir one-third of the remaining whipped cream into the peanut butter mixture until blended. Then, using a rubber spatula, gently fold in the remaining whipped cream just until no white streaks remain.

❀ Spoon the filling into the cooled pie shell. Spread the reserved whipped cream over the top of the pie, forming peaks with the back of a spoon. Lightly draw a vegetable peeler along the length of the block of chocolate to form curls. Scatter evenly over the top of the pie. Refrigerate, uncovered, for 2–6 hours. Remove from the refrigerator about 15 minutes before serving.

NUTRITIONAL ANALYSIS PER SERVING: Calories 840 (Kilojoules 3,528); Protein 20 g; Carbohydrates 47 g; Total Fat 68 g; Saturated Fat 29 g; Cholesterol 124 mg; Sodium 451 mg; Dietary Fiber 4 g

Italian Plum Cake

PREP TIME: 20 MINUTES

COOKING TIME: 1 HOUR

INGREDIENTS

1 lb (500 g) Italian prune plums, halved and pitted

1¼ cups (10 oz/310 g) granulated sugar

¾ cup (6 oz/185 g) plus 2 table-spoons unsalted butter, at room temperature

4 eggs, separated

finely grated zest of 1 orange

finely grated zest of ½ lemon

1 teaspoon vanilla extract (essence)

1½ cups (7½ oz/235 g) all-purpose (plain) flour

½ cup (2 oz/60 g) cornstarch (cornflour)

2 teaspoons baking powder

2 tablespoons Grand Marnier or other orange-flavored liqueur

1 tablespoon confectioners' (icing) sugar

SERVING TIP: For an attractive pre-sentation, place a paper doily on the cake before dusting it with confec-tioners' sugar, and then carefully lift off the doily, leaving a decorative pat-tern stenciled on top.

This simple but elegant cake filled with plums doused with Grand Marnier is a great way to end nearly any meal. The plums need not be perfectly ripe for this cake; if they are very firm, however, put them in a paper bag with an apple for a few days and they will ripen nicely.

SERVES 8–10

❀ Preheat an oven to 375°F (190°C). Butter a 9-inch (23-cm) springform pan and dust with flour, tapping out the excess.

❀ Place the plum halves in a bowl and sprinkle with ¼ cup (2 oz/60 g) of the granulated sugar. Set aside.

❀ In a large bowl, using an electric mixer set on high speed, beat together the butter and the remaining 1 cup (8 oz/250 g) granulated sugar until light and fluffy, about 5 minutes. Beat in the egg yolks, one at a time, beating well after each addition. Stir in the orange zest, lemon zest, and vanilla.

❀ In a bowl, sift together the flour, cornstarch, and baking powder. In another bowl, using the electric mixer fitted with clean beaters, beat the egg whites until stiff but not dry.

❀ Fold the flour mixture into the butter mixture in 3 batches, alternat-ing with the egg whites and ending with the whites. Do not overmix. Spread half of the batter in the prepared pan.

❀ Bake for 10 minutes. Remove from the oven and arrange the plum halves, cut sides up, on top of the prebaked batter. Sprinkle with the liqueur. Carefully spread the remaining batter evenly over the plums. Return to the oven and bake until lightly browned on top, 50–55 min-utes. Transfer to a rack to cool for 5 minutes, then run a knife around the sides of the cake to loosen them from the pan.

❀ Let cool for 45 minutes longer, then remove the pan sides. Using a small sieve, dust the top of the cake with the confectioners' sugar. Serve slightly warm.

NUTRITIONAL ANALYSIS PER SERVING: Calories 469 (Kilojoules 1,970); Protein 6 g; Carbohydrates 64 g; Total Fat 21 g; Saturated Fat 12 g; Cholesterol 144 mg; Sodium 145 mg; Dietary Fiber 2 g

stalks with slightly pink bulbs. Dry, yellow stalks have likely lost their flavor and fragrance. To release flavor, lightly bruise the stems with the side of a heavy knife blade.

MUSHROOMS, PORTOBELLO

The fully matured form of cremini mushrooms, these grow 4 inches (10 cm) or larger in diameter. When cooked, they have a rich, almost meaty taste and texture, which make them prime candidates for the grill.

MUSTARD

Mustard seeds are used primarily in two forms in outdoor cooking: ground into an intensely hot yellow powder that delivers pungent heat to many dishes; and blended with a liquid to create the common table condiment. **Dijon mustard** is made from dark brown mustard seeds (unless otherwise marked "blanc") and white wine or wine vinegar and has a distinctive pale color and moderately hot, sharp flavor.

NUTS

The mellow taste and crunchy texture of nuts complement both savory and sweet dishes. For the best selection, look in a specialty-food shop, a health-food store, or the baking section of a food market. Some of the most popular options include mellow, sweet **almonds,** commonly available skinned (blanched) and cut into slivers; **peanuts,** which are actually a legume, sometimes sold dry-roasted (cooked without oil); brown-skinned, crinkly surfaced, rich, sweet **pecans; pine nuts,** the small, ivory-colored, resinous-tasting nuts extracted from the cones of a species of pine tree; and rich, crisp **walnuts,** of which the English variety is best known and most widely available.

OILS

Nearly tasteless oils such as **safflower oil** or the richer **peanut oil** are excellent for all-purpose cooking. So, too, is **pure olive oil,** which has been blended and refined. **Extra-virgin olive oils,** by contrast, are generally fruity and full flavored; use them for dressing salads or as a condiment. **Asian sesame oil,** pressed from roasted sesame seeds, adds its nutty fragrance to both Asian and Western dishes as a seasoning or condiment. Do not confuse it with the lighter, less-flavorful cold-pressed sesame oil sold in health-food stores and well-stocked food stores. **Walnut oil,** preferably made from toasted nuts, carries the distinctive, rich taste of that popular nut. Store all oils in airtight containers at cool room temperature, away from light. Buy Asian sesame oil and walnut oil in small quantities, as they tend to turn rancid quickly.

ONIONS

The intense, prolonged heat of outdoor grills and smokers is often used to caramelize the natural sugars of onions, developing rich, mellow, sweet flavors. The varieties called for in this book include **green (spring) onions** (right), also known as scallions, which are long, slender white bulbs harvested immature, leaves and all; **Vidalia onions** (below), resembling large, flattened yellow onions, which have a sweet flesh akin to other mild varieties such as the Maui, Walla Walla, and 1015 Supersweet; small, pungent **white onions,** sometimes called boiling onions, which measure no more than about 1 inch (2.5 cm) in diameter; and **yellow onions,** the most commonly available, distinguished by their dry, yellowish brown skins and strong-flavored white flesh.

PROSCIUTTO

This cured ham is a renowned specialty of Parma, Italy, though it is produced in other regions as well. The hams are dry-salted for 1 month, then air-dried in cool curing sheds for 6 months or longer. The unique qualities of prosciutto are best appreciated when it's cut into tissue-thin slices. It may be eaten on its own or as a complement to summer fruits such as figs or melon, or it may be chopped or julienned and used in cooked dishes.

SALT, COARSE

Coarse-grained, purified rock salt, sold in the seasonings section of food stores, is frequently used in marinades, rubs, and other seasonings. Coarse salt is sometimes labeled kosher salt. More intensely flavored coarse **sea salt,** made by evaporating sea water, is an acceptable substitute in recipes calling for coarse salt.

SHALLOTS

These members of the onion family have paper-thin, copper-colored skins covering pale, purple-tinged flesh. They have a crisp texture and refined flavor that's more intense than an onion and also less hot.

SOY SAUCE

Fermented soybeans, wheat, salt, and water are the basis for this staple seasoning of Asian cuisine. The best soy sauce has a rich aroma and a taste that is both salty and mellow. Those labeled "light" are lighter in color and flavor, while "reduced-sodium" versions taste less salty.

SPICES

Derived from aromatic seeds, berries, buds, roots, or barks, a wide range of spices enlivens many grilled and smoked dishes. Buy spices in small quantities from a store that has a regular turnover of inventory, as flavors diminish rapidly. Store spices in airtight containers away from heat and light.

ALLSPICE

This sweet Caribbean spice, sold ground or as whole dried berries, gets its name because its flavor resembles a blend of cinnamon, cloves, and nutmeg.

ANISEED

This small, crescent-shaped seed of a plant related to parsley is noted for its sweet, licoricelike flavor. Aniseeds are generally sold whole, to be crushed with a mortar and pestle or a spice mill.

CAYENNE PEPPER

Finely ground from the dried cayenne chile, this powdered seasoning has a spicy-hot flavor and orange-red color.

CELERY SEED

The small, dried, pale green seed of the familiar salad vegetable. The seeds have a subtle, mild flavor reminiscent of celery stalks.

CINNAMON

One of the most popular sweet-hot spices, cinnamon is the bark of a type of evergreen tree, sold as long, thin curls (cinnamon sticks, below) or ground into a powder.

CLOVES

Native to Southeast Asia, these dried flower buds of an evergreen tree have a rich, highly aromatic flavor and may be used whole or ground in both sweet and savory recipes.

CORIANDER

The small, spicy-sweet seeds of the coriander plant; also the source of the herb known as fresh cilantro or Chinese parsley. Use coriander seeds whole or ground.

CUMIN

Sold either as whole, small, crescent-shaped seeds or ground into a pale brown powder, cumin has a strong, dusky flavor and aroma.

CURRY POWDER

The term *curry powder* describes complex Indian blends of spices, usually including coriander, cumin, ground dried chile, fenugreek, and turmeric, as well as cardamom, cinnamon, cloves, allspice, fennel seeds, and ginger.

FIVE-SPICE POWDER

This mixture, usually made up of star anise, fennel or aniseed, cloves, cinnamon, and Sichuan peppercorns, is primarily used in Chinese and Vietnamese recipes.

PAPRIKA

This powdered spice, made from the dried paprika pepper, is available in sweet, mild, and hot forms. Hungarian paprikas are generally considered to be the best quality.

RED PEPPER FLAKES

The coarsely crushed dried flesh and seeds of hot red chiles, this seasoning adds a touch of fire to sauces, marinades, rubs, dressings, and other savory recipes.

TURMERIC

This powdered spice imparts a bright yellow color and a mildly pungent, earthy taste.

SUGARS

Many barbecue sauces and marinades rely on sugar to give them characteristic sweetness. Brown sugars, which combine varying quantities of molasses with granulated sugar to yield **golden**, **light brown**, or **dark brown** sugar, are the most popular choices of barbecue chefs.

VINEGARS

The word *vinegar* literally means "sour wine," describing what results when certain strains of yeast cause wine to ferment for a second time, turning it sharply acidic. The best-quality wine vinegars begin with good-quality wine. **Red wine vinegar**, like the wine from which it is made, has a more robust flavor than vinegar produced from white wine. Vinegars are also made from other alcoholic beverages, among which **cider vinegar** is notable for its distinctive apple flavor.

WORCESTERSHIRE SAUCE

This traditional English condiment is a complex mixture of several savory and sweet ingredients, including molasses, soy sauce, garlic, onion, and anchovies. Especially well suited to red meats, it is often included in marinades and bastes, in addition to its popularity as a table sauce.

YOGURT

Noted for its mildly acidic flavor and custard-like texture, yogurt is made from lightly fermented milk. It adds mellow richness, body, and tang to a wide variety of dishes.

ZEST

The outermost, brightly colored layer of a citrus fruit's rind is rich in essential oils that flavor savory and sweet dishes alike. Citrus zest may be removed in several ways: in small particles with a fine grater; in thin strips with a swivel-bladed vegetable peeler or a special citrus stripper; or in fine shreds with the small, sharp-edged holes of a citrus zester. In every case, care should be taken not to remove any of the thick layer of bitter white pith beneath the zest.

INDEX

Asian skewered lamb 69
asparagus with Parmesan cheese 75

baby back ribs with peach sauce 72
banana licuado, pineapple- 15
barbecue sauce 46
beans, bourbon baked 82
beef
    chilied flank steak 67
    porterhouse steak with sauce rouille 63
    smoked brisket with spicy soppin' sauce 56
berries
    peach and berry shortcake 99
    strawberry-raspberry sherbet 100
    turkey breast with dried cranberry salsa 21
beverages 14–15
bok choy, cloaked fish stuffed with 50
bourbon baked beans 82
bread, corn, with chorizo 85
brisket, smoked, with spicy soppin' sauce 56
burgers, deviled turkey 40

cabbage
    Midwestern coleslaw 86
    shredding 86
cherry sauce, black, duck breasts with 42
chicken
    classic barbecued 46
    Malaysian-style, with satay sauce 34
    smoked, and fennel salad with almonds 26
    spicy, Saint Lucian style 29
    stuffed crookneck squash 93
    wings, tandoori, with raita 25
chipotle sauce, monkfish with 53
chorizo, corn bread with 85
clams
    mixed seafood grill 19
coconut shrimp with lime 37
coleslaw, Midwestern 86
corn
    corn bread with chorizo 85
    on the cob with pepper butter 97
    reviving 76
    salad, South Fork 76
Cornish hens with olive oil and rosemary 33
cranberry salsa, dried, turkey breast with 21

deviled turkey burgers 40
direct-heat method 10–11
duck breasts with black cherry sauce 42

eggplant
    ratatouille on the grill 90
equipment 108

fennel, smoked chicken and, salad with almonds 26
fire, building a 10–11
fish
    cloaked, stuffed with bok choy 50
    cooking time for 22

honey-cured smoked salmon 30
mixed seafood grill 19
monkfish with chipotle sauce 53
steaks, grilled, with tartar sauce 22
tangy salmon steaks 39
flank steak, chilied 67

grape leaves, stuffed, with dipping sauce 64
grill care 11

honey-cured smoked salmon 30

indirect-heat method 11
Italian plum cake 107

lamb
    Asian skewered 69
    leg of, with peppery mint jelly 60
    stuffed grape leaves with dipping sauce 64
lemon and lime tart 103
licuado, pineapple-banana 15
lime
    coconut shrimp with 37
    and lemon tart 103
    sparkling limeade 15

Malaysian-style chicken with satay sauce 34
mangoes
    peeling 45
    scallops and papaya with mango sauce 45
menus, planning 16–17
Midwestern coleslaw 86
mint jelly, peppery 60
monkfish with chipotle sauce 53
mushroom and spinach salad 81
mussels
    mixed seafood grill 19

papaya and scallops with mango sauce 45
peaches
    baby back ribs with peach sauce 72
    and berry shortcake 99
peanut butter pie with mocha crust 104
peanuts
    Malaysian-style chicken with satay sauce 34
    pork satay with bell pepper 59
pecan stuffing, pork chops with green chile and 70
peppers
    corn on the cob with pepper butter 97
    pork chops with green chile and pecan stuffing 70
    pork satay with bell pepper 59
    ratatouille on the grill 90
    turkey-stuffed 49
pie, peanut butter, with mocha crust 104
pineapple-banana licuado 15
plum cake, Italian 107
pork. See also prosciutto; sausage
    baby back ribs with peach sauce 72
    chops with green chile and pecan stuffing 70
    satay with bell pepper 59
porterhouse steak with sauce rouille 63
potatoes
    old-fashioned potato salad 89

rustic grilled 94
prosciutto
    stuffed crookneck squash 93

raita, tandoori chicken wings with 25
raspberry sherbet, strawberry- 100
ratatouille on the grill 90
ribs, baby back, with peach sauce 72
rice
    red, grilled shrimp and sausage with 54
    turkey-stuffed peppers 49

salads
    Midwestern coleslaw 86
    mushroom and spinach 81
    old-fashioned potato 89
    smoked chicken and fennel, with almonds 26
    South Fork corn 76
salmon
    honey-cured smoked 30
    steaks, tangy 39
sangria, red wine 14
satay, pork, with bell pepper 59
satay sauce, Malaysian-style chicken with 34
sausage
    corn bread with chorizo 85
    and shrimp, grilled, with red rice 54
    turkey-stuffed peppers 49
scallops and papaya with mango sauce 45
seafood grill, mixed, 19. See also individual seafood
sherbet, strawberry-raspberry 100
shortcake, peach and berry 99
shrimp
    butterflying 37
    coconut, with lime 37
    mixed seafood grill 19
    and sausage, grilled, with red rice 54
smoking techniques 12–13
South Fork corn salad 76
spinach and mushroom salad 81
squash
    grilled summer, with green sauce 78
    ratatouille on the grill 90
    stuffed crookneck 93
strawberry-raspberry sherbet 100

tandoori chicken wings with raita 25
tart, lemon and lime 103
tartar sauce, grilled fish steaks with 22
tea cooler, iced 14
tomatoes
    Asian skewered lamb 69
    ratatouille on the grill 90
turkey
    breast with dried cranberry salsa 21
    burgers, deviled 40
    -stuffed peppers 49

vegetables. See also individual vegetables
    ratatouille on the grill 90
    South Fork corn salad 76

zucchini. See squash

ACKNOWLEDGMENTS

The publishers would like to thank the following people and associations for their generous assistance and support in producing this book: Desne Border, Linda Bouchard, Ken DellaPenta, Hill Nutrition Associates, Cecily Upton

The following kindly lent props for photography: Fillamento, Williams-Sonoma, and Pottery Barn, San Francisco, CA. The photographer thanks Jim and Kathryn Baldwin and Candace Barnes for generously sharing their homes for location settings. He would also like to thank Chromeworks and ProCamera, San Francisco, CA, and FUJI film for their generous support of this project. Special acknowledgment goes to Daniel Yearwood for the beautiful backgrounds and surface treatments.